Sidney Lee

Stratford-on-Avon From the Earliest Times to the Death of Shakespeare

With 45 illlus. by Edward Hull

Sidney Lee

Stratford-on-Avon From the Earliest Times to the Death of Shakespeare
With 45 illlus. by Edward Hull

ISBN/EAN: 9783337009427

Printed in Europe, USA, Canada, Australia, Japan

Cover: Foto ©ninafisch / pixelio.de

More available books at **www.hansebooks.com**

STRATFORD-ON-AVON

*FROM THE EARLIEST TIMES
TO THE DEATH OF SHAKESPEARE*

BY

SIDNEY LEE

WITH FORTY-FIVE ILLUSTRATIONS BY
EDWARD HULL

NEW EDITION

LONDON
SEELEY AND CO. LIMITED, ESSEX STREET
NEW YORK: MACMILLAN & CO.
1890

CONTENTS

	PAGE
INTRODUCTORY	1
1. THE ORIGIN OF THE TOWN, AND ITS RELATIONS WITH THE SEE OF WORCESTER	8
2. AGRICULTURAL LIFE . . .	15
3. MEDIÆVAL TRADE, MARKETS, AND FAIRS	24
4. JOHN, ROBERT, AND RALPH OF STRATFORD	32
5. THE CHURCH OF THE HOLY TRINITY .	37
6. THE GUILD . . .	51
7. SIR HUGH CLOPTON'S BENEFACTIONS .	76
8. THE REFORMATION AT STRATFORD	88
9. THE GROWTH OF SELF-GOVERNMENT . .	95
10. JOHN SHAKESPEARE IN MUNICIPAL OFFICE AND IN TRADE	104
11. THE STRATFORD INDUSTRIES AND POPULATION .	111
12. JOHN SHAKESPEARE'S FIRST SETTLEMENT IN STRATFORD —THE STREETS . '	117
13. THE CONSTRUCTION AND FURNITURE OF THE HOUSES —THE GARDENS	128
14. THE SANITARY CONDITION OF THE TOWN	147
15. PLAGUES, FIRES, FLOODS, AND FAMINES .	155

Contents

		PAGE
16. Domestic and School Discipline		168
17. The Occupations of Stratford Lads		184
18. The Players at Stratford		192
19. Rural Sports		199
20. Charlecote House—Poaching in the Park		211
21. Indoor Amusements		232
22. Christenings and Marriages		243
23. Shakespeare at Stratford in Later Life		254
24. The Gunpowder Plot—Combe's Death—The Attempt to enclose the Welcombe Fields		272
25. Shakespeare's Death and his Descendants		283

LIST OF ILLUSTRATIONS

STRATFORD CHURCH, FROM THE RIVER	*Frontispiece.*
	PAGE
MEADOW WALK BY THE AVON	16
ASTON-CANTLOW CHURCH	25
THE CHURCH OF STRATFORD-ON-AVON	39
PORCH OF STRATFORD CHURCH	43
STRATFORD CHURCH, FROM THE NORTH	47
REMAINS OF THE OLD FONT AT WHICH SHAKESPEARE WAS CHRISTENED	50
THE CHAPEL OF THE GUILD OF THE HOLY CROSS	53
THE CHAPEL OF THE GUILD. INTERIOR	59
THE GUILDHALL	65
SOME REMAINS OF THE OLD BUILDING AT THE REAR OF CLOPTON HOUSE	79
STRATFORD BRIDGE	85
STAIRCASE OF CLOPTON HOUSE	87
LUDDINGTON VILLAGE AND NEW CHURCH	93
SHAKESPEARE'S BIRTHPLACE BEFORE RESTORATION	118
SNITTERFIELD CHURCH	121
THE RED HORSE HOTEL	129
THE ROOM IN WHICH SHAKESPEARE WAS BORN	135

List of Illustrations

	PAGE
THE UPPER STORY OF SHAKESPEARE'S BIRTHPLACE	139
THE BIRTHPLACE OF SHAKESPEARE	145
OLD HOUSES IN ROTHER STREET	149
THE HOUSE OF DR. JOHN HALL	157
OLD LYCH-GATE AT WELFORD	163
AN OLD ALE-HOUSE, STRATFORD-ON-AVON	169
THE GRAMMAR SCHOOL	179
MARY ARDEN'S COTTAGE AT WILMECOTE	205
CHARLECOTE PARK	217
THE GRAND HALL AT CHARLECOTE	223
ARMS OF LUCY	231
BIDFORD	233
HILLBOROUGH	239
STRATFORD, FROM THE SOUTH-EAST	244
ANNE HATHAWAY'S COTTAGE AT SHOTTERY. INTERIOR	247
ANNE HATHAWAY'S COTTAGE AT SHOTTERY	251
OLD CHURCH OF LUDDINGTON	253
APPROACH TO SHOTTERY, FROM STRATFORD	259
CLIFFORD CHURCH AND OLD HOUSES	267
THE CLOPTON PEW	273
MEMORIAL OF SIR HENRY RAINFORD IN CLIFFORD CHURCH	276
OLD GRAVESTONES IN THE CHURCHYARD OF STRATFORD-ON-AVON	285
SHAKESPEARE'S MONUMENT	289
CHANCEL OF THE CHURCH OF THE HOLY TRINITY, STRATFORD	293
THE SHAKESPEARE MEMORIAL THEATRE, STRATFORD-ON-AVON	297
THE CHANCEL OF STRATFORD CHURCH	301
DISTANT VIEW OF STRATFORD-ON-AVON	303

STRATFORD-ON-AVON

INTRODUCTORY

"ONE thing more," wrote Sir William Dugdale in 1657, at the close of the eighteen folio pages of his *Antiquities of Warwickshire* devoted to Stratford-upon-Avon, "one thing more in reference to this ancient town is observable, that it gave birth and sepulture to our late famous poet, Will Shakespeare." There is little need to add the comment that the "one thing more," about Stratford, which the learned antiquary thought to have adequately noticed in these four-and-twenty words, has grown into the only thing about it that most men now regard as memorable. Nor would the modern pilgrim —that is, he who makes his pilgrimage with fitting judgment—readily admit that Dugdale has indicated the highest points of interest about Shakespeare's connection with Stratford. That the borough was his birthplace and burial-place gives it, after all, a smaller attraction than that he lived there for full two-thirds of his life. And completely as the resources of civilisation have remodelled the town in many of its aspects, it still boasts sufficient survivals of the age of Elizabeth to give the sojourner a far-off glimpse of Shakespeare's daily environment. The nineteenth-century manufacturer has not set his mark upon it: the inhabitants know little of life at high pressure. Their acknow-ledged affinity with the hero who makes their life worth living in more than a single sense, would seem to have held them aloof from all the ruder currents of modern life. It is only within the last half century that the town has begun to extend its boundaries, and the extension has not yet attained very gigantic measurements. The chief streets, with their offshoots, although they have grown wider in many places and in all cleanlier, still bear the names by which Shakespeare knew them. The church on the river bank has undergone little change, and time has dealt very kindly with the exterior of the ancient Chapel of the Guild, with the

Guildhall, and with the Grammar School, all of which were once overlooked by the windows of Shakespeare's far-famed house, at the meeting of Chapel Street with Chapel Lane. Although that house has gone, the public garden christened after it New Place occupies the exact site of the "great garden" that surrounded it when the poet was its owner. Cross-timbered houses, with the carved front in one instance at least merely mellowed by the lapse of years, often break the monotony of unlovely stretches of modern brickwork. The stone bridge across the Avon is in all its essentials the same as when the Elizabethans crossed it. The watermill, although shaped anew, continues to do the noisy work in which it has persevered through nine centuries.

And when once the town is deserted for Shakespeare's playing fields in the neighbouring country, the changes grow less marked. Stratford always stood upon a "plain ground," as Leland described it early in the sixteenth century, surrounded by "the champain," that is, the flat open country. The woodland has grown scantier, but there is still no lack of it on the low hills of the district, and here and there on the banks of the river. The Forest of Arden, which was in its decadence in Elizabethan England, has now retreated into a mere name, but it was always in historic times cut off from Stratford by a wide enough tract of land to prevent it from affecting materially the immediate scenery. The Avon itself winds as of old from Naseby to the Severn, with Stratford on its right bank, midway between its source and mouth, and at a little distance from Stratford it still flows under bridges at Binton and Bidford which are as authentic relics of the sixteenth century as their fellow at Stratford. Numberless villages, like Shottery and Snitterfield, pursue that drowsy rural life which seems always able to resist time's ravages. They have not grown: some of them have been renovated by the modern builder; in a very few cases they have fallen into decay and all but disappeared. But none have quite reached *la fin du vieux temps*; and the preservation of an occasional relic like the maypole on the village green at Welford suggests to the least thoughtful passer-by their near relationship with the past. Saunter where we will by the homesteads and meadows of South

Warwickshire, we are still led from time to time within view of scenes which may well have inspired poetic passages like Perdita's invitation to the sheep-shearing feast, or the song of Spring in *Love's Labour's Lost.*

But there is some danger, although the practice is an attractive one, in making Shakespeare's name the central feature of all Stratford history and topography. It has been done too often already. The writers of guide-books or monographs on the town and district have always endeavoured to fix the attention of the pilgrim or student exclusively on points of Shakespearian interest, and have valued only as much of their investigations as belongs to Shakespearian lore.

The scraps of information that their labours have yielded are of their kind beyond price; but they fail to enable the reader to form a coherent conception of the town's general development or social growth. With all respect to the antiquaries of Stratford, it may be said that they have overlooked facts in the various stages of the history of the borough which are of striking importance in the municipal history of the country. Nor is this the limit of their offence, if offence can justly be used in such a context. Although it would be only by an awkward distortion of the neglected facts that they could be turned to account in Shakespeare's biography, those of them that relate to the Middle Ages undoubtedly offer us traditions which influenced the life and thought of the poet as a Stratford townsman of greater receptivity than his neighbours; while those that concern the late years of the sixteenth century, or the early years of the seventeenth, can be made to create for us a picture of the society in which he actually moved. Thus we may be brought to the conclusion that something of Dugdale's method of dealing with Stratford is not without its advantages for the Shakespearian student. It is possible that an account of the town that shall treat it as a municipality not unworthy of study for its own sake, and shall place Shakespeare among its Elizabethan inhabitants as the son of the unlucky woolstapler of Henley Street or as the prosperous owner of New Place, will be more suggestive and in better harmony with the perspective of history, than a mere panegyric on the parochial relics as souvenirs of the poet's birthplace, home, or sepulchre. The following pages are intended as an experiment in the former direction.

I

THE ORIGIN OF THE TOWN, AND ITS RELATIONS WITH THE SEE OF WORCESTER

THERE are many towns in England that can claim greater antiquity than Stratford-on-Avon.[1] The county of Warwickshire, called by Drayton (himself a Warwickshire man) the heart of England, was doubtless in prehistoric ages part of the vast forest which covered all the Midlands, and which survived in later times in the chain of wood stretching, with occasional clearings, from Byrne Wood in Buckinghamshire, through Abingdon and Wych Woods in Oxfordshire, to the forests of Dean, Arden, Cannock, and Sherwood, and the Derbyshire

---

[1] The main authority for the history of mediæval Stratford is Dugdale's account of the town in his *History of Warwickshire*, first published in 1656, and reissued under the editorship of Dr. William Thomas in 1718. Kemble's *Codex Diplomaticus* gives the text of the charters noted below.

Wolds. The discovery of a very few tumuli in the district, containing some rude stone implements, mark the presence of a very sparse population in a neolithic age.

Avon is the Celtic word for river, which as *Afon* is still good Welsh. Arden is formed from the Celtic *ard*, high or great, and *den*, the wooded valley—a compound which also supplied Luxemburg with its district of the Ardennes. Place-names like these prove the sojourn of Celtic tribes in the north and south of Warwickshire before the Roman occupation. The Romans bestowed the title *Cornavii* on the inhabitants of the county. We know nothing of its origin, and find few traces of Roman civilisation in the district. But Rome's ubiquitous roadmakers did not leave the neighbourhood untouched. Ryknield Street, which ran from Tynemouth in Northumberland, through York, Derby, and Birmingham, to St. David's, skirted the Forest of Arden on its west side; passed through Studley and Alcester, and left the county five miles below Stratford by way of Bidford. The name of *Straetford* is a proof, too, that this was not the only "street" which approached the site of Stratford. It must have started into being like five other villages in different parts of England similarly named, as the approach of a Roman *street* to a *ford*—as the approach to a ford across the Avon of the smaller Roman road that ran from Birmingham through Henley-in-Arden to London. But whether it had become an inhabited place, or had its name before the Romans left Britain, is mere matter of conjecture.

Of the Teutonic settlers, a Saxon tribe, known to history as the Hwiccas, occupied Warwickshire and its neighbourhood in the sixth century; but according to local legends, the Celts did not make way for them without a struggle, which was waged very fiercely up the Welcombe Hills that overlook Stratford. For some years the Hwiccas lived in independence under their own alderman; but in the seventh century they were absorbed within the great Marchland — the middle kingdom of Mercia — and their aldermen declined into mere agents of the Mercian kings. The see of Worcester was formed about 679, and all the district of the Hwiccas constituted the bishop's diocese.

The Origin of the Town

The seventh century all but closes without supplying us with any authentic details as to the rise of Stratford. The earliest documentary clue to its origin is to be gleaned from a charter dated 691, according to which Egwin, the third Bishop of Worcester, obtained from Ethelred, King of Mercia, "the monastery of Stratford," standing on land above three thousand acres in extent, in exchange for a religious house that the bishop had erected at Fladbury, in Worcestershire. The best critics have doubted the authenticity of the document, but another charter of unblemished reputation, dated nearly a century later, supports its statements, and leads to the inference that Stratford owes its foundation to a monastic settlement. In 781 Offa, the great King of Mercia, confirmed, after much discussion, the right of Heathored, the Bishop of Worcester, to "Stretforde," then an estate of thirty hides; and in 845 another ruler of Mercia absolutely surrendered to another bishop the Stratford monastery by the Avon, to be held by him and his successors free of all secular obligations. This is the latest glimpse we obtain of this foundation, and it, perhaps, afterwards fell into decay. The Bishops of Worcester, like many others of their profession, doubtless found it more to their interests to foster a new village, and to cultivate the land about it, than to maintain monks who could not readily be turned to profit. According to tradition, this early monastery stood on the site where the church stands now, and, as in many other parts of England, the first houses at Stratford were probably erected for its servants and dependents. Their abodes were doubtless near the river, in the street that has for many centuries been known as "Old Town."

The Saxon Bishops of Worcester were evidently proud of their Stratford property, and they sought with success to extend its boundaries in all directions. Records prove that the land was rich in meadows, pastures, and fisheries, and was well watered by shallow brooks. It was at no distant date that the bishop's original property, which included only the immediate environment of the monastery, obtained the name of Old Stratford, to distinguish it from a newer Stratford-on-Avon, which stretched far along the north bank of the Avon. Thanes, who were the country gentlemen of Anglo-Saxon society, willingly rented under agreements for two or three lives large plots of ground of the bishop, and a few neighbouring villages retain in their nomenclature traces of this occupation. Alveston, originally called Eanulfestun, was the homestead of Eanulf, its tenant in 872, under Bishop Wearfrith. Bishopston (Bishopestune) was doubtless the site of a small homestead erected for the bishop's own residence. All the fertile land about Clifford was let in 988 to a Thane Ethelward.

Thus, before the Norman Conquest, Stratford had become a valuable portion of the property of the see of Worcester; and in this condition of dependence it remained till the Middle Ages closed. It appears to have been little disturbed by any of the political convulsions that overwhelmed many parts of Anglo-Saxon England in the ninth and tenth centuries. The Danes may have threatened it from a distance while passing from the conquest of Mercia into Wessex, on their first great expedition; but little is known of their route. There can be little doubt that the tale of Warwick's legendary hero, Guy, embodies some authentic tradition of a Mercian warrior who successfully resisted the Danish invaders in the tenth century. Perhaps to him the Stratford townsfolk may have owed their immunity from the second invasion of his kinsmen in the tenth century; and he may have at times come among them on returning from hunting or hawking in the Forest of Arden, of which his friend and tutor Harald or Heraud, according to the popular romance, was a native.

It is certain that the Norman Conquest passed almost silently over South Warwickshire, and Stratford showed little sign of its passage. Its lord at the time was Bishop Wulfstan, who was famed for his holy life, and was alone of all the Anglo-Saxon prelates rewarded for his ready acquiescence in the new dominion with continuance in his office. He proved his gratitude by twice leading his militia, his county tenants, some of whom doubtless came from Stratford, in battle against the Norman king's enemies — once against the half-Breton Earl of Hereford, who sought to escape from William's yoke during his absence in Normandy in 1074, and once near Worcester against rebels from the Welsh border.

II

AGRICULTURAL LIFE

IN 1085 the first distinct account of Stratford was put on record by the Domesday surveyors, and it supplies us with many interesting details.[1] The district had then been for several centuries one of the Bishop of Worcester's *manors*, and all the manorial machinery was at work upon it. The township growing up there was a village community, consisting mainly of very small farmers and a few day-labourers with their families, and in all their relations of life the inhabitants were under the jurisdiction of the bishop's steward, or seneschal, in virtual serfdom. He presided over the manor court, constituted as the court baron, to which the townsmen came

---

[1] See Domesday Survey (Record Commission). Mr. Seebohm's invaluable book on *The Village Community in England* (1883) has defined the conditions of mediæval agriculture.

to supervise the payments of rent and dues, the settlement of new-comers, and the distribution of land. He, too, kept order in the villages, and, with the aid of the community assembled in court leet, punished breaches of the peace.

MEADOW WALK BY THE AVON.

He saw that the land was properly cultivated, that the ploughs were fully yoked, and that the seed was fairly sown.

The actual extent of Stratford in William I.'s time was fourteen and a half hides, or nearly 2000 acres. It was of smaller extent than it had been under the Mercian *régime*, for

Agricultural Life

the neighbouring villages had now themselves become so many separate manors. The inhabitants consisted of a priest, who, doubtless, conducted services in the chapel of the old monastery, with twenty-one villeins and seven *bordarii*. Each of these residents was the head of a family, and their number, therefore represents a population of about one hundred and fifty. The villeins stood the higher in the social scale.

On all sides of the village lay arable land, divided by balks of earth into narrow strips, each about half an acre in size. Each villein held, besides his homestead, strips of this land, sometimes amounting in the aggregate to sixty acres, but the strips in one ownership seldom adjoined each other, being scattered over all the fields adjoining the village. The *bordarii*, from the Saxon *bord*, a cottage, were cottagers who owned a cottage with a garden, and some five acres in strips distributed as in the case of the villeins over the fields at hand. But every householder, whether villein or cottager, evidently possessed a plough. The community owned altogether thirty-one ploughs, of which three belonged to the bishop, the lord of the manor, and were probably drawn by a team of eight oxen. Both classes of residents were liable to small money payments to the lord of the manor, and occasionally to payments of agricultural produce, besides being called upon to labour for several days every year on portions of the land cultivated in the bishop's own behalf. There was very little meadow land. The Domesday surveyors only found one field of that character five furlongs long and two broad. All the energies of the inhabitants were clearly engaged in growing wheat, barley, and oats. By the river at the same time stood the water-mill belonging to the bishop. There the villagers were obliged to grind all their corn, and they had to pay a fee for the privilege. In 1085 the mill produced an income of ten shillings annually, but the bishop was often willing to accept eels in discharge of the mill-fee, and a thousand eels were usually sent to Worcester year by year by the customers of the village mill. It is noticeable that the total profit derived from Stratford by Wulfstan was £25 in the Domesday Survey, an amount five times that derived from it in the days of Edward the Confessor. The advance marks the rapid progress of the settlement in the interval.

In the century and a quarter (from 1085 to 1210) following, the village does not seem to have made any giant's strides. Alveston, the obscure little village that now lies in the bend of the river nearest to Stratford in its upward course, seemed likely then to rival it in prosperity. Just before the Norman Conquest, "certain great men," says Dugdale, had withheld Alveston from the Bishops of Worcester after it had long been in their possession, but William the Conquerer restored it to Bishop Wulfstan, who generously made it over to the great Worcestershire Priory. Throughout the Middle Ages that religious foundation rivalled the see itself in the possession of broad lands. Three mills were erected beside the Avon at Alveston, and eels without number were sent year by year by its inhabitants to the refectory of the priory. The boundaries of the Alveston Manor crept up in the thirteenth century to their still existing limits on the southern side of the bridge of Stratford (it was a rude wooden bridge at this early date), and the manorial officers planted a little colony by their end of the bridge, which was known to them and to the Elizabethans as Bridgetown. Its dwellers were all of them *bordarii* or cottagers, and in the descriptive rental of the Worcestershire Priory compiled about 1250,[1] the names and annual dues, which varied from five shillings to sixteenpence, are given at length. One was called Brun, another John de Pont (or, as we should say, John Bridge), another William Cut. The steward, or seneschal, who looked after this, with much surrounding property, was a native of Stratford, Nicholas by name, who held a messuage there with a garden besides arable land in three neighbouring fields. For his house and land he had to pay sixpence quarterly, to cut hay in the meadow belonging to the lord of the manor for one day, and to help in stacking it, besides spending three days in reaping his lord's grain.

The various services and payments due as rent from the husbandmen of Stratford and its neighbourhood at the time—services which seemed to increase in intricacy with the centuries—are given at length in the book

---

[1] *Cf.* the *Custumary of the Worcestershire Priory*, published by the Camden Society.

of the possessions of the Worcestershire Priory, and illustrate the life led by the majority of the villagers in the infancy of the town. Of the changes in the condition of the inhabitants since the Domesday Survey, it need only be noted that many of the large estates outside the town had been let as knight's fees, that is to say, on condition of their holders performing certain military services, and that some of the villeins within the village had become free tenants (*libere tenentes*), that is to say, men free from the imputation of serfdom, who were permitted to cultivate their land as they would, and paid for their farms a fixed money rental, with little or no labour services to supplement it. But the majority of the inhabitants were still villeins or cottagers, and labour services were exacted from both these classes with vexatious regularity. Villeins who owned sixty acres had to supply two men for reaping the lord's fields, and cottagers with thirty acres supplied one. On a special day an additional reaping service was to be performed by villeins and cottagers with all their families except their wives and shepherds. Each of the free tenants had then also to find a reaper, and to direct the reaping himself. Happily on that occasion the steward saw that all the labourers were fed at the cost of the manor. The villein was to provide two carts for the conveyance of the corn to the barns, and every cottager who owned a horse provided one cart, for the use of which he was to receive a good morning meal of bread and cheese. One day's hoeing was expected of the villein and three days' ploughing, and if an additional day were called for, food was supplied free to the workers. Villeins and cottagers were also expected to assist in cutting the hay, in carting and stacking it. When the hay had all been gathered in, each householder was to be presented with a ram, a fourpenny cheese, and a small sum of money instead of the fodder to which they were of old allowed to help themselves. No villein nor cottager was permitted to bring up his child for the Church without permission of the lord of the manor. A fee had to be paid when a daughter of a villein or cottager married. On his death his best waggon was claimed by the steward in his lord's behalf, and a fine of money was exacted from his successor—if, the record wisely adds, he could pay one. Any townsman who made beer for sale paid for the privilege. But these charges exhausted the manorial demands. Fishing was free, church dues were small, and the mills and the barns for storing grain were at times placed freely at the disposal of the population.

III

MEDIÆVAL TRADE, MARKETS, AND FAIRS

BUT although agricultural pursuits chiefly occupied the people of Stratford in the thirteenth century, several of them also turned their attention to trade, and in an account of the settlement rendered to the Bishop of Worcester about 1251, we can trace the rise of several industries that acquired importance later. There were already numerous weavers, tanners, and tailors. There were carpenters and dyers, whitesmiths and blacksmiths, wheelwrights and fleshmongers, shoemakers and coopers. The mill employed a number of labourers as millers and fullers.[1]

The Bishops of Worcester were clearly anxious to encourage such pursuits. Before

---

[1] *Cf.* a survey of Stratford made for the Bishop of Worcester in 1251, privately printed by Sir Thomas Phillipps at the Middlehill Press.

the close of the twelfth century they obtained for the town from Richard I. the special privilege of a weekly market upon the Thursday, a privilege for which the citizens paid the bishops an annual toll of sixteen shillings. At first the

ASTON-CANTLOW CHURCH.

Thursday market was with difficulty maintained, and it almost died within a century of its birth. But in 1314 it was reinaugurated, and became a permanent feature of Stratford mediæval life.

The pasture-land within and without the manorial boundaries must have grown since the date of the Domesday Survey, for cattle was certainly a staple commodity of the earliest Stratford market. From time immemorial one of the chief thoroughfares in the town has been known by its present name of Rother Market, and it was doubtless there that the first market was held. *Rother* represents the Anglo-Saxon word "Hreother," *i.e.* cattle (from the Teutonic "Hrinthos," whence the modern German *rind*). The ancient word long survived in Warwickshire, and was familiar to Shakespeare, who employed it in the line, "The pasture lards the rothers' sides."[1] It is a more significant mark of commercial progress that early in the thirteenth century the various dues of such inhabitants as were anxious to engage in trade were commuted by the lord of the manor for a fixed annual sum of twelvepence, payable quarterly. The holdings of these traders consisted of little more than a house and very small gardens, and were known as burgages, while their holders were called burgesses. Such a tenure bore, in the west of England, the name of "the custom of Bristol," a commercial port only second in importance at the time to London; and its introduction

[1] *Timon of Athens*, IV. iii. 12.

into Stratford proves the growth of mercantile pursuits.

Meanwhile the national records do not concern themselves with Stratford very much. The Hundred Rolls of Edward I., which were drawn up in many counties to form a survey as complete as that of the Domesday Book, barely deal with Warwickshire; and all they tell us concerning Stratford is that the king's justices had regulated by standard the manufacture of beer in the town, and that the steward of the Bishop of Worcester had not enforced the regulation. The entry adds that John, a clergyman and bailiff of the Bishop of Worcester, had taken ten shillings from a man of Aston-Cantlow, doubtless a political offender, who was in prison at Stratford, as a bribe to permit him to escape. Both these illegal episodes are dated after the battle of Evesham. They seem to imply some local discontent. Perhaps the people of Stratford, or the bishop's steward there, had not favoured Henry III's cause in his contest with the barons, or it may be that the law had fallen into contempt amid the confusion into which the Midlands were plunged by the strife which closed in favour of the king at Evesham in 1265.

Further commercial privileges were conferred upon the town at frequent intervals in the thirteenth century. Stratford was then endowed with a series of annual fairs, the chief stimulants of trade in the middle ages. As early as 1216 a grant was obtained by the Bishop of Worcester for the holding of a yearly fair, "beginning on the eve of the Holy Trinity"—*i.e.* on the Saturday following Whitsuntide—"and to continue for the two next days ensuing." Other fairs were added as the century progressed. In 1224 a fair was permitted on the eve of St. Augustine, the 26th of May, "and on the day and morrow after." In 1242 and in 1271 a similar distinction was conferred on both the eve of the Exaltation of the Holy Cross—14th of September—"the day, and two days following," and "for the eve of the Ascension of our Lord, commonly called Holy Thursday, and upon the day and morrow after." The grant of the earliest fair on Trinity Sunday was renewed in 1272, and in mediæval times it always proved the busiest of the four gatherings, although that of the Holy Cross in September has continued longest. Early in the following century permission was secured by the townsfolk to hold another fair for the long period of fifteen days, to begin yearly on the eve of St. Peter and St. Paul, at the latter end of June. Out of each of these celebrations the Bishop of Worcester made an annual profit of about nine shillings and fourpence.

The choice of Trinity Sunday for the earliest of the Stratford fairs was doubtless due to the facts that the parish church was dedicated to the Holy Trinity, and that Trinity Sunday being "the festival of the church's dedication," had at Stratford, as in other parts of the country, long been celebrated by a "wake," which brought many neighbouring villagers to the town. The spiritual side of mediæval life had a tendency to merge itself in the worldly side, and there is nothing exceptional in a Sunday of specially sacred character being turned to commercial uses. In most mediæval towns, moreover, traders exposed their wares at fair-time in the churchyard, and chaffering and bargaining were conducted in the church itself. The Statute of Winchester attempted in vain in 1285 to restrain this extravagance, but it persisted till the Reformation. In an early printed "Comment on the Ten Commandments by way of dialogues between Dives and Pauper" (1493), the "profane custom" is forcibly condemned. Dives asks Pauper, "What sayest thou of them that hold markets and fairs in Holy Church and in Sanctuary?" Pauper replies, "Both the buyer and the seller, and men of Holy Church that maintain them, or suffer them when they might let [*i.e.* hinder] it, be accursed. They make God's house a den of thieves." To which Dives answers, "And I dread me that full often by such fairs God's house is made a tavern of gluttons. For the Merchants and Chapmen keep there with them their wives and lemans both night and day." The riotous times spent at Stratford a century later, when the fairs were in process, makes this a very pertinent description.

Thus the close of the thirteenth century guaranteed the future prosperity of Stratford. The rivalry with Alveston was then practically over, and its development was assured. The Bishops of Worcester had shown themselves exceptionally vigilant over its interests, and it was proving year by year more profitable to them. In 1251 the arable land returned to them more than £40; in 1299 more than £57.

Mediæval Trade, Markets, and Fairs

The mills had grown in number; there were three for grinding corn by the river, and one for fulling elsewhere. They yielded at times as much as £13 : 6 : 8, an enormous increase on their ancient profits. Arable, meadow, and pasture all became richer with cultivation. The lords of the manor found it convenient to make a park in the neighbourhood for hunting purposes, and therefore paid it frequent visits. One bishop anticipating Justice Shallow, and not always with more effect, threatened all who "broke his park and stole his deer" with excommunication.

IV

JOHN, ROBERT, AND RALPH OF STRATFORD

In the fourteenth century the inhabitants were no longer solely dependent for their welfare on the benevolence of the lords of the manor. Villenage gradually disappeared in the reign of Edward III, and all who were not burgesses became free tenants or copyholders, paying definite rents for house and land. And from these classes sprang men capable of stimulating the prosperity of their birthplace by their own exertions. Three fourteenth-century prelates, one of whom rose to be Archbishop of Canterbury, and the two others to be Bishops respectively of London and Chichester, were natives of Stratford, and in days when the principle of personal nomenclature was still unsettled, borrowed of the town their surnames. John of Stratford, Robert of Stratford, and Ralph of Stratford were closely related. The two former were brothers, and Ralph was their nephew.

Robert, the father of the prelates Robert and John, was a well-to-do inhabitant of Stratford, who appears to have set his sons an example in local works of benevolence. He it is to whom has been attributed the foundation, in 1296, of the chapel of the guild—that is, of the religious fraternity of which we shall speak hereafter—and of the hospital or almshouses attached to it. But the benefactions of his sons and his grandson were in many points more remarkable, and are better known to authentic history.

There is little need to pursue their careers in detail here; but they gave so practical an effect "to a more than ordinary affection" for the town, that Stratford must always honour their memory. It must always be profitable, too, to study their lives as illustrating the rich opportunities of advancement in the political and ecclesiastical worlds open in the middle ages to ability, even when revealing itself in the sons of village farmers. John and Robert were both for a time Chancellors of England, and there is no other instance in English history of that high dignity falling to two brothers in succession.

All three were educated at the Universities, and successes there proved stepping-stones to preferment in Church and State. Ralph obtained a canonry at St. Paul's, which led to the bishopric of the metropolis. The latter office he held from 1340 to 1354, and during his episcopate he rented a house in "Bruggestret," or Bridge Street, Stratford.[1]

Robert's first benefice was the living of Stratford itself, bestowed on him by the Bishop of Worcester in 1319, and in that office he was the earliest of the three relatives to give tangible form to his regard for his birthplace. Long streets were in the course of formation at Stratford in the reign of Edward II. One ran from the Holy Trinity Church towards the northeast. Henley Street, whence Henley-in-Arden could be most readily reached, had tenements on both sides of it; and Greenhill Street, afterwards Moor Town's End, had, like Old Town, long been inhabited thoroughfares. Robert resolved to roughly pave these roads. By obtaining permission in 1332 to impose

[1] *Corporation Records*, vol. i. p. 1.

a toll for four years "on sundry vendible commodities," brought by the agriculturists of the neighbourhood into the town, "he defrayed the charge thereof," and the tax was renewed for short periods, at his suggestion, in 1335 and 1337, after he had left the city to exercise higher dignities. From the Archdeaconry of Canterbury he was promoted in 1337 to the see of Chichester. But, like his brother John, he aimed at political advancement as well as ecclesiastical, and twice filled the office of Chancellor of England. He survived both his distinguished brother and nephew, dying in 1362.

John of Stratford, the most eminent of the three, made a name at Oxford by his knowledge of civil law, was Bishop of Winchester from 1323 to 1333, and became in the latter year Archbishop of Canterbury.[1] He played a prominent part in the politics of his time. As Bishop of Winchester, he drew up the Bill of Deposition against Edward II, and Marlowe gives us a glimpse of him in the most pathetic scene in his play of *Edward II.* He undertook more foreign embassies than any of

[1] See Hook's *Lives of the Archbishops of Canterbury.*

his contemporaries, and could boast of thirty-two journeys made across the Channel in the public service. It was John of Stratford who, after Edward III left England on his first French expedition in 1338, virtually governed the country as Lord Chancellor. Twice already had he filled that dignified office. But the king was dissatisfied with the small amount of money that his councillors now managed to collect for his wars, and suddenly returned in 1341 to dismiss all his ministers, charging them with dishonesty in their offices. The archbishop boldly denied Edward's accusation, and bade him remember his father's fate, and the rights of the people of England. The king had at length to yield to John of Stratford, who takes his place in English history as a sturdy defender of the constitution.

V

THE CHURCH OF THE HOLY TRINITY

THE most notable benefactions which Archbishop John of Stratford, before his death in 1348, conferred on Stratford were gathered about the parish church. The church, although at the time, as the evidence of some of the stonework proves, a substantial erection, was not fully completed. It had even then many architectural pretensions. The tower still retains its Normanesque panel arches, with their Early English lights, which probably date from the farther side of 1200. But John of Stratford desired to make the structure more stable and more elaborate. Although cruciform in shape, it had but an embryo south aisle, and the north aisle was very narrow. Having widened the north aisle, the archbishop placed there a chapel to the Holy Virgin, and the Bishops of Worcester promoted the decoration of the chapel by granting indulgences to those who contributed money towards the expenses. The south aisle the archbishop built anew, and in it he set up a chapel in honour of St. Thomas à Becket, with whom he had some qualities in common. The church tower he renovated, and probably added the wooden spire, with which Shakespeare and his contemporaries were acquainted. But his work was not wholly confined to mere structural improvements.

In 1332, with the permission of the Bishop of Worcester and Edward III, John of Stratford formed a chantry of the chapel of the church, dedicated to St. Thomas the Martyr. It is difficult for some of us nowadays to appreciate the spirit that prompted such a foundation. The archbishop's object was to endow five priests to chant for all time at the altar of this chapel masses for the souls of the founder and his friends. John of Stratford, who had acquired much property about Stratford, appointed for the maintenance of the priests of his chantry one messuage in Stratford, with the Manor of

Inge, the modern Ingon-by-Welcombe, and among those whose souls his masses were expected to free from purgatory were, besides himself, his brother Robert, his father and mother, the Kings of England, and the Bishops of Worcester. Of the five priests, one was to be warden of the chapel and another sub-warden. John of Stratford, in spite of his political cares, watched over the chantry with paternal affection. Year by year he added land and houses in Stratford to its possessions, and his friends followed his example. One of these was Nicholas of Dudley, parson of King's Swynford, in Worcestershire, a connection of a family with a notorious career before it, who made over much property to the chantry about his native village of Dudley. And the patronage of the church of Stratford, John purchased of the Bishop of Worcester, and gave to his chantry priests, who thus fully controlled the parish church.

Ralph of Stratford was not behind his uncles in his generosity to his native town. In 1351 he built for John's chantry priests a "house of square stone for the habitation of these priests, adjoining to the churchyard." The ten carpenters and ten masons, with the labourers, who doubtless came from London to erect the edifice, were placed, while at Stratford, under the king's special protection. The building came to be known as the College of Stratford, and was familiar to the Elizabethans and their successors, as the map of 1769 amply proves. In 1415 Henry V confirmed all the privileges of the chantry and the college, and the church of Stratford then bore the honoured epithet of collegiate, since it was under the supervision of a college or chapter of priests, in much the same manner as Westminster Abbey and St. George's Chapel, Windsor, are to this day.

Other inhabitants of Stratford followed the example set by the three prelates of Stratford, and made many sacrifices to adorn their church. True penitents were urged by the Bishop of Worcester in 1321 to contribute to the building and the repair of the belfry, and in 1381 to adorn and illuminate the altar of the Virgin Mary. The warden of the college in the time of Edward IV, Dr. Thomas Balsall, "added a fair and beautiful choir, rebuilt from the ground

PORCH OF STRATFORD CHURCH.

at his own cost," which still survives. He clearly employed master masons of different schools. One was faithful to the older models, and especially to the Early Decorated style. Of his work are the tomb of Balsall, who died in 1491, the north and south doors, and, doubtless, the font at which Shakespeare was baptized. The other artificer aimed at greater novelty. He studied his bestiary, and perched paunchy toads on buttresses, or transferred dragon-flies in grotesque attitudes to stone cornices. His angels are very whimsical, and if the carvings in the stalls be his, he delighted in picturing the least refined aspects of humanity. Ralph Collingwood, the warden at the close of the fifteenth century, gave the collegiate church its final touches. He renewed the north porch and the nave. "The low decorated clerestory was removed, the walls pulled down to the crowns of the arches, rude angels (by some 'prentice hand) were inserted to carry the pilasters, and the walls were panelled with large lantern windows, with a flattish roof."[1]

In pursuit of Dr. Balsall's "pious intent," Collingwood improved the church service

[1] Knowles's *Architectural Account of Holy Trinity Church.*

by appointing "four children choristers, to be daily assistants in the celebration of divine service," and placed them under the supervision of the college; "which choristers," according to Collingwood's ordination, "should always come by two and two together into the choir to Matins and Vespers on such days as the same were to be sung there, according to the Ordinale Sarum; and at their entrance into the church, bowing their knees before the crucifix, each of them say a Pater Noster and an Ave. And for their better regulation did he order and appoint that they should sit quietly in the choir, saying the Matins and Vespers of our Lady distinctly, and afterwards be observant in the offices of the choir: that they should not be sent upon any occasion whatsoever into the town: that at dinner and supper they should constantly be in the college to wait at the table: and to read upon the Bible or some other authentic book: that they should not come into the buttery to draw beer for themselves or anybody else: that after dinner they should go to the singing school: and that their schoolmaster should be one of the priests or clerks appointed by the discretion

STRATFORD CHURCH FROM THE NORTH.

of the warden, being a man able to instruct them in singing to the organ: as also that they should have one bedchamber in the church, whereunto they were to repair in winter-time at eight of the clock, and in summer at nine: in which lodging to be two beds, wherein they were to sleep by couples: and that before they did put off their clothes they should all say the prayer of *De profundis* with a loud voice, with the prayers and orisons of the faithful, and afterwards say thus, 'God have mercy on the soul of Ralph Collingwood, our Founder, and Master Thomas Balsall, a special benefactor to the same.'" For the maintenance of the choristers, lands were assigned at Stratford, Binton, and Drayton.

Shakespeare only knew Stratford after the Reformation had stripped it of all these ecclesiastical distinctions—distinctions which were so many tributes of affection paid to their birthplace by his ancient fellow-townsmen—but the majority of them had been solidly embodied in stone, with which time in his day had not dealt unkindly. They were monuments enshrining traditions not wholly lifeless, and may well have helped a poet to realise the setting of scenes like

King John's death under the windows of Swinstead Abbey, or Gaunt's last moments in Ely House.

Remains of the old Font at which Shakespeare was christened now in the Vestry of Stratford Church.

E. Hull Oct. 24th 1883.

VI

THE GUILD

But mediæval life at Stratford in the later Middle Ages developed a new feature, which gives it by far its greatest attraction to the student of English municipal history. Self-government was in the Middle Ages the aim of every English town which deserved the name; but so far as our investigations have led us, the townsmen of Stratford had made no advance in that direction. Before the fourteenth century closed, however, an institution had arisen and taken formal shape in their midst, which was to deprive the Bishops of Worcester of their ancient authority. The Guild, that then went by the triple name of the Holy Cross, the Blessed Virgin, and St. John the Baptist, and which still gives its name to the picturesque chapel in Church Street, embodied this emancipating influence. It very possibly represents the union of three distinct guilds, each bearing one of the names cited; but we have no historical evidence of their combination, and for our present purpose it is sufficient to regard it as a single institution.[1]

The early English guilds must not be confounded with the modern survival in the city of London. The guilds owed their origin to popular religious observances, and developed into institutions of local self-help. They were societies at once religious and friendly, "collected for the love of God and our soul's need." Members of both sexes—and the women were almost as numerous as the men—were admitted on payment of a small annual subscription. This primarily secured for them the perform-

[1] Ample materials for the history of the Stratford Guild are to be found in "Stratford-on-Avon Corporation Records—The Guild Accounts," by Mr. Richard Savage, reprinted from the Stratford-on-Avon *Herald* for 1885. This is a calendar of the extant accounts for the fourteenth and fifteenth centuries, which was prepared at the expense of Mr. Charles Flower of Stratford. Mr. Savage has prepared for publication another collection of guild documents preserved at Shakespeare's birthplace, Stratford. See also Toulmin-Smith's "*Documentary History of English Guilds*," published by the Early English Text Society, Mr. J. C. Jeaffreson's "Report on the Stratford University," published in the Eighth Report of the Historical MSS. Commission, and Thomas Fisher's extracts from the Guild Records which appeared in the *Gentleman's Magazine* for 1835.

THE CHAPEL OF THE GUILD OF THE HOLY CROSS.

ances of certain religious rites, which were more valued than life itself. While the members lived, but more especially after their death, lighted tapers were duly distributed in their behalf, before the altars of the Virgin and of their patron saints in the parish church. A poor man in the Middle Ages found it very difficult, without the intervention of the guilds, to keep this road to salvation always open. Relief of the poor and of necessitous members also formed part of the guild's objects, and gifts were frequently awarded to members anxious to make pilgrimage to Canterbury, and at times the spinster members received dowries from the association. The regulation which compelled the members to attend the funeral of any of their fellows united them among themselves in close bonds of intimacy.

But the social spirit was mainly fostered by a great annual meeting. On that occasion all members were expected to attend in special uniform. With banners flying they marched in procession to church, and subsequently sat down together to a liberal feast. The guilds were strictly lay associations. Priests in many towns were excluded from them, and, where they were admitted, held no more prominent places than the laymen. The Guilds employed mass priests to celebrate their religious services, but they were the paid servants of the fraternity. Every member was expected to leave at his death as much property as he could spare to the guilds, and thus in course of time they became wealthy corporations. They all were governed by their own elected officers—wardens, aldermen, beadles, and clerks—and a common council formed of their representatives kept watch over their property and rights.

Although these religious guilds did not concern themselves with trade, in many instances there grew up under their patronage smaller and subsidiary guilds, each formed of members engaged in one trade, and aiming at the protection of their interests in their crafts. Under the name of craft-guilds, these offshoots often, as in London, survived the decay of the religious association; their pedigrees became obscured and they were credited with greater originality and antiquity than they could justly claim. Guilds of the religious kind can be traced far back in Anglo-Saxon times. King Ine and

King Alfred mention them in their legal codes. But the thirteenth and fourteenth centuries saw their palmiest days. Chaucer includes some of their members among his Canterbury pilgrims.

> An Haberdasher and a Carpenter,
> A Webbe, a Deyer, and a Tapiser,
> Were all y-clothed in o livere
> Of a solempne and grete fraternite.
>
> . . . . .
>
> Wel semed eche of hem a fayre burgeis,
> To sitten in a gild halle, on the deis.
> Everich, for the wisdom that he can,
> Was shapelich for to ben an alderman.

At Stratford the guild claimed a very ancient history. "The guild has lasted," wrote its chief officers in 1389, "and its beginning was, from time whereunto the memory of man reacheth not." Its muniments now collected in the birthplace at Stratford prove that it had been in existence early in the thirteenth century, and that bequests were then made to it. William Sude, who lived in the reign of Henry III, is the name of the author of the earliest extant deed of gift, and he gave a messuage of the yearly value of sixpence. Many of his contemporaries are known to have followed this example, for the sake of their own souls or those of their fathers and mothers. The Bishops of Worcester encouraged such gifts, and apparently contrived that some of the guild's revenues should be devoted to the relief of poor priests ordained by them without any sure title. Godfrey Giffard, on 7th October 1270, issued letters of indulgence for forty days to all sincere penitents who had duly confessed their sins, and had conferred benefits on the Guild of the Holy Cross of Stratford-on-Avon. Before Edward I.'s reign closed the guild was wealthy in houses and lands. In 1353, from which year the extant account-books date, there was scarcely a street in Stratford without a house belonging to the association.

It was in Edward I.'s time that the elder Robert of Stratford laid for the guild the foundation of a special chapel, and of neighbouring almshouses. These buildings, with the hall of meeting, called the Rode or Rood Hall (rood being equivalent to cross), were doubtless situated in Church Street, where the guildhall and guild buildings subsequently stood, as they stand at this day. The fourteenth century witnessed a rapid growth of the guild's prosperity. In 1332 Edward III gave the corpora-

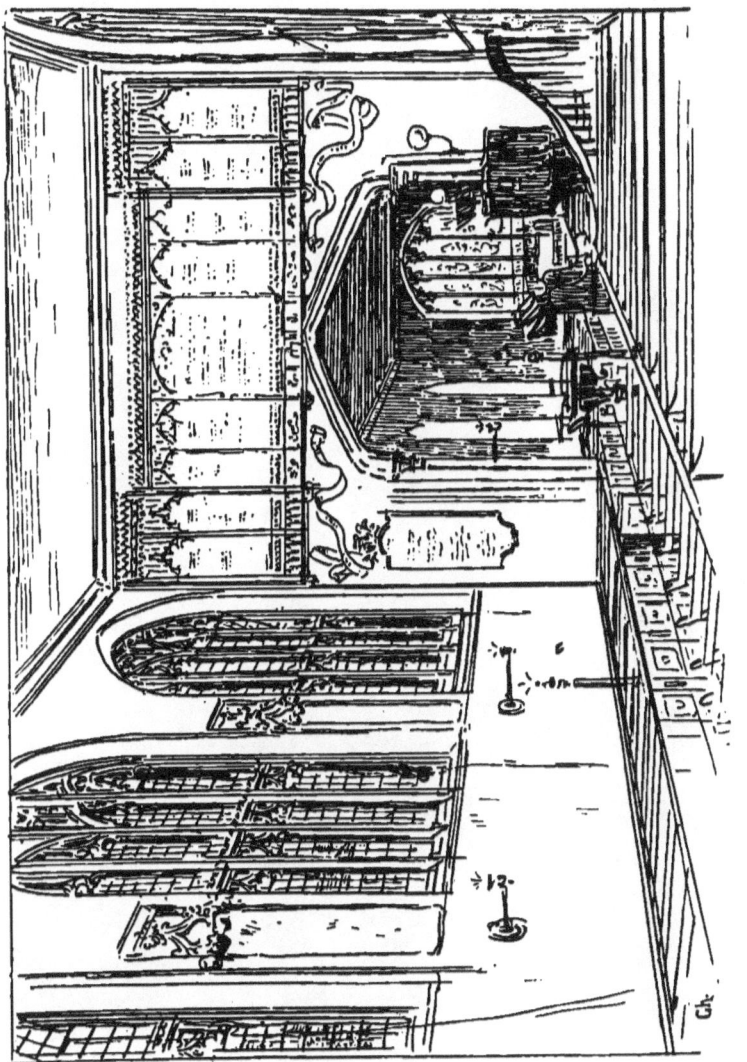

THE CHAPEL OF THE GUILD. INTERIOR.

The Guild

tion a charter which confirmed its right to all its possessions, and to the full control of its own affairs. In 1389 Richard II sent commissioners to report upon the ordinances of the guilds throughout England, and the return for Stratford is still extant, though the historians of the town have persistently overlooked it. The details are so picturesque that I make no apology for quoting them in full.

These are the ordinances (the document begins) of the brethren and sisters of the Guild of the Holy Cross of Stratford.

First: Each of the brethren who wishes to remain in the guild, shall give fourpence a year, payable four times in the year; namely, a penny on the feast of St. Michael, a penny on the feast of St. Hilary, a penny at Easter, and a penny on the feast of St. John Baptist. Out of which payments there shall be made and kept up one wax candle, which shall be done in worshipful honour of our Lord Jesus Christ and of the blessed Virgin and of the Holy Cross. And the wax candle shall be kept alight every day throughout the year, at every mass in the church, before the blessed Cross; so that God and the blessed Virgin, and the venerated Cross, may keep and guard all the brethren and sisters of the guild from every ill. And whoever of the brethren or sisters neglects to come at the above-named times [when the payments are due], shall pay one penny.

It is also ordained by the brethren and sisters of the guild, that, when any of them dies, the wax candle before-named together with eight smaller ones, shall be carried from the church to the house of him that is dead; and there they shall be kept alight before the body of the dead until it is carried to the church; and the wax candles shall be carried and kept alight until the body is buried, and afterwards shall be set before the Cross. Also, all the brethren of the guild are bound to follow the body to church, and to pray for his soul until the body is buried. And whoever does not fulfil this, shall pay one halfpenny.

It is also ordained by the brethren and sisters, that if any poor man in the town dies, or if any stranger has not means of his own out of which to pay for a light to be kept burning before his body, the brethren and sisters shall, for their souls' health, whosoever he may be, find four wax candles, and one sheet, and a hearsecloth to lay over the coffin until the body is buried.

It is further ordained by the brethren and sisters, that each of them shall give twopence a year, at a meeting which shall be held once a year; namely, at a feast which shall be held in Easter week, in such manner that brotherly love shall be cherished among them, and evil-speaking be driven out; that peace shall always dwell among them, and true love be upheld. And every sister of the guild shall bring with her to this feast a great tankard; and all the tankards shall be filled with ale; and afterwards the ale shall be given to the poor. So likewise shall the brethren do; and their tankards shall, in like manner, be filled with ale, and this also shall be given to the poor. But, before that ale shall be given to the poor, and before any brother or sister shall touch the feast in the hall where it is accustomed to be held, all the brethren and sisters there gathered together shall put up their prayers, that God and the blessed Virgin and the venerated Cross, in whose honour they have come together, will keep them from all ills and sins. And if any sister does not bring her tankard, as is above said, she shall pay a halfpenny. Also, if any brother or sister shall, after the bell has sounded, quarrel, or stir up a quarrel, he shall pay a halfpenny.

It is also ordained, that no one shall remain in this guild unless he is a man of good behaviour.

It is moreover ordained, that when one of the brethren dies, the officers shall summon a third part of the brethren, who shall watch near the body, and pray for his soul, through the night. Whoever, having been summoned, neglects to do this, shall pay a halfpenny.

It is ordained by the Common Council of the whole guild, that two of the brethren shall be Aldermen; and six other brethren shall be chosen, who shall manage all the affairs of the guild with the Aldermen; and whoever of them is absent on any day agreed among themselves for a meeting, shall pay fourpence.

If any brother or sister brings with him a guest, without leave of the steward he shall pay a halfpenny. Also, if any stranger, or servant, or youth, comes in, without the knowledge of the officers, he shall pay a halfpenny. Also, if any brother or sister is bold enough to take the seat of another, he shall pay a halfpenny.

Also, if it happens that any brother or sister has been robbed, or has fallen into poverty, then, so long as he bears himself well and rightly towards the brethren and sisters of the guild, they shall find him in food and clothing and what else he needs.

These ordinances, providing for kindly gifts of beer to the poor, for the preservation of good fellowship among all the members and for their participation in each others' joys and griefs, vividly put before us the simple piety and charity of the Stratford townspeople. The regulations for the government of the guild by two wardens or aldermen and six others prove the progress of the town in the direction of self-government. It is not difficult to perceive how an association, which grew to include all the substantial householders of the district, necessarily acquired much civil jurisdiction; how its members referred to its council their disputes with one another; how the aldermen were gradually regarded as the administrators of the municipal police; or how the burgesses preferred this new *régime* to servile dependence on the steward of the lord of the manor. The college priests were very jealous of the guild's growing influence, and when the guild resisted the payment of tithes brought a lawsuit against it to compel their payment. But this seemed to be the fraternity's only external obligation.

The ledgers or account-books of the guild, still extant for the fourteenth and fifteenth centuries, well repay close study. Their microscopic details enable the historian to trace the progress of the society in all its aspects

THE GUILDHALL.

from year to year and almost from month to month.

The receipts under the various headings of "light-money," rents, and fines increase with satisfactory regularity, and the expenses grow correspondingly. Candles both of tallow and wax, repairs of house property, the setting up of hedges, form large items of expenditure, but in each year's balance-sheet the details of the food and drink provided for the annual feast occupy more and more extravagant space. The small pigs and large pigs; the pullets, geese, veal, and "carcases" of mutton; the eggs, butter, and honey; the almonds, raisins, currants, garlic, salt, pepper, and other spices were gathered in from all the neighbouring villages in appalling quantities. Gallons of wine and bushels of malt for brewing ale were likewise provided in generous measure. Horsemen were often equipped at the guild's expense to bring in the supplies. After the feast was done there came the settlement for such items as washing the napery, rushes for the floor of the dining hall, coal and charcoal for the kitchen, the cooks' and other servants' wages. At times the feast was enlivened by professional minstrelsy. Twenty pence was paid to minstrels from Warwick in 1424 and a single performer was often engaged at a fee of fivepence.

The guild buildings, the chief room of which was the guildhall, were enlarged and embellished after 1400. A parlour was added in 1427; it was paved with tiles, and the window was of glass. A chimney was provided for the counting-house at the same time and a school-house was built. The building material all came from neighbouring places—tiles from Warwick, stone from Drayton or Grafton, plaster from Welcomb. Additions were also made to the almshouses set up near at hand for the guild's pensioners, and towards the close of the fifteenth century the chapel was carefully repaired. Meanwhile the number of the members steadily increased. One curious feature of the later conditions of membership was that the souls of the dead could be made free of the fraternity on payment from the living as easily as the living themselves. Thus, early in the fifteenth century six persons surnamed Whittington, the dead children of John Whittington, of Stratford, were all admitted to a share in the guild's spiritual benefit for the sum of ten shillings. Before the Middle Ages closed, the fame of the guild had grown wide enough to attract to its ranks noblemen like George, Duke of Clarence, Edward IV's brother, and his wife, with Edward, Lord Warwick, and Margaret, two of their children; and so distinguished a judge as Sir Thomas Lyttleton was one of the members. Merchants of towns as far distant as Bristol and Peterborough joined it, and few towns or villages of Warwickshire were unrepresented on its roll of members. All the neighbouring clergy were prominent members.

The fee for admission at its flourishing epochs varied from six shillings and eightpence to four pounds, according to the wealth of the candidates. Those artificers and traders unable to pay the entrance fee in money were allowed to defray it in work. Thus, in 1408 Simon Gove, carpenter, was admitted on his undertaking to build a porch at the door of the guild, and in 1409 John Iremonger was admitted on covenanting to build a house on the guild ground, at the end of Henley Street. Five years later John Ovyrton, a cook, of Warwick, and his wife, were received into the fraternity on condition of cooking the annual dinner, for which they were to receive the hood of the

guild—the chief part of its distinctive uniform—
and their expenses. In 1427 several weavers
were made free of the guild on condition of
supplying cloth for the members' hoods and a
banner with paintings on it. In other years,
building material—tiles, plaster of Paris, stone
—was taken instead of the fees. Gifts in kind
from the prosperous members were frequent.
Silver cups, silver spoons, ecclesiastical vestments, missals, statues of saints, and wax for
candles were often presented by novices. Con-
tributions to the annual feasts of corn, malt,
salt, white or red wine, were always welcomed.
In 1416 the guild received from five members
"a great pot for frumetty, a broad dish of
mascolyn, one basin, one board-cloth, and
one towel"; and in 1426 eight couples of
rabbits, two ewes with lamb, and a boar. In
1421 the presents included a silver chalice
and a coat of armour, and in 1474 seven
pewter dishes and ten pewter saucers. A
schedule of "the diverse goodes and juellies
beynge in the Gildehalle" in 1434 is remarkable for the number and richness of its
contents. Nor was there any falling off
in the bequests of houses and lands. The

guild acquired in 1481 the rectory and chapelry of Little Wilmecote, where the Ardens—the ancestors of Shakespeare's mother—had property with all its tithes and profits. In 1419 a tenement in Church Street, and in 1478 a shop in the Middle Row, came into its possession, and later nearly all High Street and Chapel Lane—then called Dead Lane or Walker Street—owned the guild as landlord.

The inner constitution did not undergo much alteration until late in the fifteenth century. New ordinances were promulgated in 1444; and while they define with more precision than the former ones the duties of the guild's officers, and the mode of election to them, they differ from their predecessors mainly in the increased importance attached to the priests or chaplains, now five in number, employed by the guild, and perhaps prove that its ancient independence of ecclesiasticism was in jeopardy. The chaplains were to perform five daily masses hour by hour, from six o'clock to ten in the morning. They were to live together in one house, under as strict a discipline concerning hours for sleep and meals as the choristers in the college by the churchyard.

They had to walk in procession with the guild in their copes and surplices, with crosses and banners, on the four principal feasts of the year, and to officiate with the priests of the college at the funeral of every member and of the pensioners in the almshouses. They were to avoid the county wakes, and not to say mass out of Stratford without the guild's permission. The guild had now its master, aldermen, and proctors elected yearly. Every new member was to be admitted in the presence of the master, the clerk, and at least two aldermen. No member could be chosen alderman unless he had first served the office of proctor. The proctors were, on the Monday following the nativity of St. John the Baptist (24th June), to receive and account for the silver money received for providing candles, and all the rents of the guild. They were to make an annual inventory of the property. Their duties also included the repair of all the tenements of the Corporation, and the arrangements for the feasts and dinners, of the dates of which they were duly to inform the members. There were more dinners than of old. Private entertainments were given to neighbouring landlords. In 1463 the Bishop of Worcester was the guest of the guild, with Sir John Greville and other persons of distinction. The master and aldermen met in council every quarter-day at least, and absentees without excuse were fined forty pence. The master saw to the purchase of cloth for the members' hoods. The oath taken on admission was to the effect that the brother or sister would truly pay his fine; that he would seek in all things the profit of the fraternity; that he would refer all his disputes with fellow-members to the master; and that he would sue none of his brethren without leave of the master and aldermen, upon pain of a fine of twenty shillings. The date of the annual feast was altered to the 6th July, the day of St. Peter and St. Paul. Several regulations were issued later to prevent the "great inconvenience and hurt that grow to this guild by private affection and grant of the master and part of his brethren," by which land and houses were let at low rents to favoured friends.

By far the most important of the new objects of the guild in the fifteenth century was the organisation of the grammar school for the children of the members. We have seen that the schoolhouse was built in 1427. Thomas Jollyffe is the name of the member always associated with its foundation, but it is now proved to have been in existence before the date (1453) usually assigned to its origin. Attendance was free, and the schoolmaster was forbidden to take anything from his pupils. The master of the guild paid him an annual salary of ten pounds. It was at the guild school, somewhat altered in shape, that Shakespeare was afterwards educated.

When the fifteenth century closed the days of the guild's prosperity were numbered. It had grown inconveniently wealthy, and its wealth was administered by a narrow oligarchy. Men and women of position in all parts of the country had sought and obtained admission to it, but the extension of the guild's boundaries was not favourable to the simple fraternal sentiment, and the duties of membership acquired a chilling formality. Religious feeling was declining, and the steady growth of the priests' influence in the guild's internal economy failed to attract new members. The fee charged for admission fell gradually from twenty-five shillings to twenty-five pence, and yet candidates decreased. To the commercial progress of the country the decline may be in part attributed. Subsidiary guilds or companies, formed of men engaged in the same or cognate trades, had risen up among the members of the old Stratford guild, and had separated the great fraternity into small cliques. At first the parent guild appears to have encouraged the formation of these traders' unions. We know that one room of the guild buildings, where "John Smyth, *alias* Colyere, first made a clock, having the hand towards the street and figures all gilded," was known as the Drapers' Chamber as early as 1419, and was probably so called because the Stratford drapers were permitted to assemble there to regulate their business arrangements. Other trades soon secured the same privilege, and in the sixteenth century every commercial pursuit had its company at Stratford. When the old religious guild was dissolved, these trade-societies or craft-guilds lived on and shared some of its traditions and repute.

VII

SIR HUGH CLOPTON'S BENEFACTIONS

At the close of the Middle Ages, the town of Stratford-on-Avon looked back on some seven or eight centuries of continuous progress. Originally the offshoot of a monastery, it had almost reached the dignity of an independent township. Bishops had nurtured it in its infancy and the discipline of religion had left its mark on the town. The majestic church with its college of priests testified to the pious benefactions of many generations of townsmen. Religion too had developed among all the inhabitants — men and women — a fraternal sentiment powerful enough to call into being the guild, which, with its hall, chapel, school, almshouses, was barely less notable from the architectural point of view than the collegiate church. If the Stratford community, less

Sir Hugh Clopton's Benefactions

fortunate than their Coventry neighbours, had failed to develop a special industry, all the simple crafts were practised in the town, and were well organised among themselves. Stratford undoubtedly felt some of the effects of the transition from the mediæval to the modern era. The guild—the centre of the town's mediæval life—temporarily suffered collapse, but it was quickly restored to a new and healthier career as the governing body of the town, and its new birth secured for Stratford municipal independence. Of outward change Stratford between the fifteenth and the eighteenth centuries knew little. Not only the chief public buildings, but many of the dwelling-houses with which Shakespeare was familiar, dated from the mediæval period, and survived far beyond Shakespeare's day. Very early in the sixteenth century some additional adornments were made by private benefactors. But when these were completed, Stratford was at all points the Stratford that Shakespeare and his children knew.[1]

From the neighbouring village of Clopton

[1] For the early part of the sixteenth century, Jeaffreson's Report, Toulmin-Smith's *Account of the Guilds*, and Dugdale are the chief authorities.

came to Stratford, about 1480, Sir Hugh Clopton, the last of its early benefactors, and to him the town owed the latest structural improvements. His biography offers many points of interest. He energetically devoted great abilities to commerce and to commercial speculations, and is noted as an early example of the self-made merchant. His pedigree is traced back to Robert of Clopton, a substantial yeoman, who in 1228 obtained from Peter de Montfort, apparently a relative of the great Simon, the Manor of Clopton, about a mile to the northeast of Stratford. Of the ninth generation in descent, Hugh was a younger son. His elder brother, Thomas, who inherited the family estates and the great Clopton Manor House, was religiously inclined, and built, in the first instance, an oratory in his manor-house, and afterwards a "fair chapel," in which he obtained Pope Sixtus IV's permission to celebrate divine service.

Hugh turned his attention at an early age to trade, and made his fortune as a mercer in London. He was Lord Mayor in 1492, never married, and devoted his leisure and his wealth to philanthropy. Stratford was his country

SOME REMAINS OF THE OLD BUILDING AT THE REAR OF CLOPTON HOUSE.

Sir Hugh Clopton's Benefactions

home. There he erected, about 1483, "a pretty house of brick and timber, wherein he lived in his latter days," and obtained lands in other parts of the town, and in Wilmecote and Bridgetown. His "pretty house," the chief building in the town, was, within the first quarter of the sixteenth century, known as New Place, and became Shakespeare's property in 1597. It stood in Chapel Street, at the corner of Chapel Lane, and at the opposite corner of the lane was the chapel of the guild. Clopton hoped to end his days there, and in his will stated his desire to be buried "in the parish church of Stratford within the chapel of our lady, between the altar there and the chapel of the Trinity." But the fates were against the fulfilment of his hope, and, dying in London in 1496, he finally "bequeathed" his body to the chapel of St. Katherine, in the parish church of St. Margaret, Lothbury.

New Place was far from being Clopton's sole contribution to Stratford. The chapel standing over against his house, and belonging to the guild, of which he was a prominent member, needed restoration in the last days of the fifteenth century, and he readily defrayed the expenses of the work. He did not touch the chancel, which was renovated about 1450, but the nave he determined to rebuild. Death overtook him before the structure was finished, but by his will he provided for its completion. "And whereas," he wrote, "of late I have bargained with one Dowland and divers other masons for the building and setting up of the Chapel of the Holy Trinity, within the town of Stratford-on-Avon aforesaid, and the tower of a steeple to the same, I will that the said masons sufficiently and ably do and finish the same with good and true workmanship, and they truly perform the same, making the said works as well of length, and breadth, and height, such as by the advice of mine executors, and other divers of the substantialest and honest men of the same parish, shall and can be thought most convenient and necessary; and all the aforesaid works to be done by mine executors, and paid upon my proper goods and charges; and in like wise the covering and roofing of the same chapel with glazing, and all other furnishments thereunto necessary to it, to be paid by my said executors as the works aforesaid goeth forth." The "furnishments" included elaborate paintings on the roof, illustrating the history of the Holy Cross. Although in mediæval times that history was usually traced back to the creation of the world, Clopton's artists connected it with no more ancient personages than King Solomon and the Queen of Sheba, and thence brought it by several stages to the time of St. Helena, the mother of Constantine, who made a successful pilgrimage to Palestine to discover its whereabouts in the fourth century. Other paintings commemorated St. Thomas à Becket, St. George and the Dragon, and the Last Judgment. In 1804 the paintings were discovered beneath a covering of whitewash, and they were copied and engraved, but they have since been more than once recoated with whitewash, and are probably wholly destroyed.[1]

Another of Sir Hugh Clopton's benefactions was of greater practical utility. The townspeople had long felt the need of a good bridge over the river, and "the great and sumptuous bridge upon the Avon, at the east end of the town," constructed of freestone, with fourteen

[1] *Cf.* Thomas Fisher's *Series of Ancient Allegorical . . . Paintings . . . discovered . . . at Stratford-on-Avon,* London, 1807, fol.

arches, and "a long causeway" of stone, "well walled on each side at the west," was erected by Sir Hugh. Leland, the antiquary, who visited Stratford about 1530 on a tour through England, noted in his account of his journey the great value of this gift. "Afore the time of Hugh Clopton," he wrote, "there was but a poor bridge of timber, and no causeway to come to it, whereby many poor folks either refused to come to Stratford when the river was up, or coming thither stood in jeopardy of life." The bridge required frequent repair, as we shall see, in Shakespeare's day, but enough of it is still standing to convince us of the workmanlike thoroughness with which its foundations were laid.

By Sir Hugh Clopton's will Stratford largely benefited in other ways. "He bequeathed also C marks to be given to xx poor maidens of good name and fame dwelling in Stratford, *i.e.* to each of them five marks apiece at their marriage; and likewise C*l.* to the poor householders in Stratford; as also L*li.* to the new building the cross aisle in the Parish Church there" (Dugdale). The testator did not, at the same time, forget the needs of the poor of

STRATFORD BRIDGE.

Sir Hugh Clopton's Benefactions 87

London, or their hospitals; and on behalf of poor scholars at the Universities, he established six exhibitions at Cambridge and Oxford, each of the annual value of four pounds for five years.

STAIRCASE OF CLOPTON HOUSE.

VIII

THE REFORMATION AT STRATFORD

ALTHOUGH the town was thus structurally completed, its internal government had not advanced with the times. The steward of the Bishop of Worcester, the lord of the manor, was still in name the supreme authority. The Reformation gave the needful impulse and exerted a determining influence on the constitutional development of Stratford. Before the Reformation had run its full course, it brought to fruition the townspeople's desire for self-government.

The new movement respected none of the old rights of ecclesiastics to property, and the claims of the Bishops of Worcester to manorial rights in Stratford were summarily set aside. About 1550 John Dudley, Earl of Warwick, one of Edward VI's Lord Protectors, and afterwards Duke of Northumberland, was installed in the bishop's place as Lord of the Manor of Stratford, and the king added to this estate the Lordship, Manor and Castle of Kenilworth, which was not very far distant. When the Duke of Northumberland's ambitious plot to set his daughter-in-law Lady Jane Grey on the throne of England came to nought, and he paid the penalty of failure on the scaffold, Queen Mary humanely made Stratford over for a short while to his widowed duchess; but she finally assigned it to the Savoy Hospital beyond Temple Bar, which she had revived for the poor of London. Such changes in the ownership of the manor did not, however, very nearly affect the townsmen; for the manorial property had been diminished by gifts of the Bishops of Worcester to the guild, and the powers of the manorial lord had been lessened by the assumption of many of his ancient functions by the fraternity's wardens and aldermen.

More important to the townsmen were the laws of Henry VIII's reign, dealing with religious houses and corporations. The Acts for their dissolution immediately affected more than one institution at Stratford. The college —the home of the chantry priests—was the first to fall. In 1535 commissioners visited it, and found the warden, the five priests, and the four choristers living there sumptuously. Subsidiary chapels had been set up by the college in the neighbouring villages of Bishopston and Luddington, of which they owned the tithes. Its lands were under the supervision of a steward and a bailiff. The annual income was £128 : 9 : 1. In 1545 another report was made, and it was noted that all its officers had, besides a good yearly stipend, two shillings weekly for their diet allowed out of the possessions of the institution. It was rich in silver and gold, and Henry VIII appropriated, before the close of his reign, no less than 260 ounces of its plate. The priests were apparently permitted to reside within the college till 1547, but in that year all college chantries and free chapels were finally suppressed. For four years the Stratford College seems to have been uninhabited. In 1551 it was made over as a royal gift to the Earl of Warwick, the new lord of the manor. He transformed it into a private residence; but his execution in 1553 brought the building again into the hands of the Crown. Elizabeth leased it in 1576 to a Richard Coningsby, and he it was who sublet it to wealthy John Combe, who lived there on good terms with Shakespeare, although he bore the reputation of being a "devilish usurer."

The guild underwent a far more striking transformation. The politicians who surrounded Henry VIII and Edward VI found the destruction of religious corporations not more satisfactory to their consciences than to their purses. In 1545 and in 1547 commissioners came to Stratford to report upon the possessions and constitution of the Guild of the Holy Cross. The income was estimated at £50 : 1 : 11½, of which £21 : 6 : 8 was paid as salary to four chaplains. There was a clerk, who received 4s. a year; and Oliver Baker, who saw to the clock (outside the chapel), received 13s. 4d. "Upon the premises was a free school, and William Dalam, the schoolmaster, had yearly for teaching £10." "There is also given yearly," the report runs, "to xxiiij poor men, brethren of the said guild, lxiijs. iiijd.; vz. xs. to be bestowed in coals, and the rest given in ready money; besides one house there called the Almshouse; and besides v or vj*li.* given them of the good provision of the master of the same guild." In the report of 1547 the importance of the guild chapel to the town is strongly insisted upon. It was more centrally situated than the parish church, since the town had long left the banks of the river, and the old and sick regularly attended service there. The chapel stood in the midst of the town, "for the great quietness and comfort of all the parishioners there; for that the parish church standeth out of the same town, distant from the most part of the said parish half a mile and more; and in time of sickness, as the plague and such like diseases doth chance within the said town, then all such infective persons, with many other impotent and poor people, doth to the said chapel resort for their daily service."

But in 1547 all these advantages ceased: the guild was dissolved, and all the property came into the royal treasury. It was, as we have seen, in the same year that the lordship of the manor was transferred from the Bishops of Worcester to the Protector Northumberland, who was far too occupied with affairs of state to renew the worn-out machinery of manorial government. And now too all the functions of local government which the guild had tacitly exercised were paralysed. For six years the town lacked any responsible government.

LUDDINGTON VILLAGE AND NEW CHURCH.

IX

THE GROWTH OF SELF-GOVERNMENT

But the inconvenience of anarchy, barely tempered by the occasional appearance of the steward of the manor, was felt to be an unbearable humiliation. About 1550 the leading townsmen—the old officers of the guild—laid their grievances before the king, and begged him to rehabilitate the guild as a municipal corporation. The application was successful, and Edward VI's reply, dated 7th June 1553, unreservedly placed the government of the borough in the hands of its own inhabitants.

Whereas (the charter ran) the borough of Stratford-upon-Avon, in the county of Warwick, is an ancient borough, in which borough a certain guild was in former time founded and endowed with divers lands, tenements, and possessions, from whose rents, revenues, and profits a certain Grammar School was maintained and supported for the education and instruction of boys and youths, and a certain charitable house was there maintained and supported for the sustenance of twenty-four poor persons, and a certain great stone bridge called Stratford Bridge, placed and built over the water and river of the Avon beside the said borough, was from time to time maintained and repaired. And the lands, tenements, and possessions of the same guild have come into our hands and now remain in our hands. And whereas the inhabitants of the borough of Stratford aforesaid from time beyond the memory of man have had and enjoyed divers franchises, liberties, and free customs, jurisdictions, privileges, reversions, and quittances by reason and pretext of charters, concessions, and confirmations made in ancient time by our progenitors to the masters and brethren of the aforesaid guild and otherwise, which the same inhabitants of the same borough aforesaid are now very little able to have and enjoy, because the aforesaid guild is dissolved, and in consideration of other causes now apparent to us whence it appears likely that the borough aforesaid and the government thereof may go to a worse state from time to time, if a remedy be not quickly provided. On which grounds the inhabitants of the borough of Stratford aforesaid have humbly prayed us that we would accord them our favour and abundant grace, for the amelioration of the said borough and the government thereof, and for the support of the great works which they from time to time are compelled and ought to sustain and support, and that we would deign to make, reduce, and create them the same inhabitants into a body corporate and politic.

And directions followed ordering this "reduction" and "creation" to proceed without delay.

Thus the ancient guild did not lie long in

cold obstruction; in 1554 it entered on a new tenure of life. The names and functions of its chief officers were slightly changed, but the bailiff, chosen on the Wednesday next before the Nativity of our Lady (8th September), was merely the old warden newly spelt. The aldermen bore the same titles as of old. The proctors were replaced by the chamberlains. The clerk's and beadle's offices remained unchanged. The common council continued to meet monthly in the guildhall or one of the adjoining chambers "at nine o'clock of the forenoon," summoned by the bell of the guild chapel; but the assembly now included, besides the bailiff and ten aldermen, the ten chief or capital burgesses, and its edicts governed the whole town. Regular performance of duty was secured by fines of six-and-eightpence on all absentees from meetings of the council, and of ten pounds on any councillor declining to assume the office of bailiff when elected to it. Very heavy penalties (five pounds for a first offence, ten for a second, and "to be expulsed" for ever for a third) punished those who discussed "forth of the council chamber" any of its proceedings. "In all and every general procession," every councillor, according to "orders passed" in 1557, was to take part "in his honest apparel as in his gown"—a survival of the hood of the guild—on pain of a twelvepenny fine, and a like forfeiture awaited any one who attended a "hall" without "his gown upon his back." The characteristic fraternal sentiment of the original institution was perpetuated in the orders "that none of the aldermen nor none of the capital burgesses, neither in the council chamber nor elsewhere, do revile one another, but brotherlike live together, and that after they be entered into the council chamber, that they nor none of them depart not forth but in brotherly love, under the pains of every offender to forfeit and pay for every default, vj$s$. viij$d$." Similarly, when any councillor or his wife died, all were to attend the funeral "in their honest apparel, and bring the corpse to the church, there to continue and abide devoutly until the corpse be buried."

The estates of the guild, to which the greater part of the college lands were added, became the corporate property, and the chattels of the guild — the vestments, armour, and plate — passed into the hands of the new body. The school, in which Edward VI showed a special interest, became, with the chapel and almshouses, institutions of the borough. The vicar of the parish church was a corporate officer, with a salary of twenty pounds annually and two pounds in tithes. Nearly all functions that the steward of the lord of the manor had performed were absorbed in the new *régime*, and for their due exercise a few new legal and police offices were created. The bailiff was a duly-appointed magistrate. He attended the judges at the assizes, and presided, with his sergeants and constables, in a monthly court of record, for the recovery of small debts, and at the great law-days or leets, to which all the inhabitants were summoned to revise and enforce the police regulations. The leets were held twice a year—on the Wednesdays after the feast of St. Michael the Archangel (29th September) and after Low Sunday, *i.e.* the week after Easter. Shakespeare was familiar with these observances. Kit Sly, talking in his sleep, promises to present the ale-wife of Wincot at the leet, "because she brought stone jugs and no seal'd quarts"; and Iago speaks in metaphor of keeping "leets and law-days." The new corporation also assumed the duty of supervising the trade of the town. Under the shadow of the religious fraternity, we have watched the trading companies come into being, and the town council now kept them strictly under its own control. The bailiff confirmed indentures of apprenticeship, and the chamberlains demanded a fee on the admission of a new member into a craft or mystery. Prices of bread and beer were fixed by the corporation, and ale-tasters were annually appointed to enforce orders as to the quality and price of victuals. Searchers were also nominated to inspect the tanneries, and to prevent the common abuses in the preparation of leather which were prohibited by statutes of the realm in 1566 and 1603.[1]

It is essential for the student of the social history of Stratford to grasp clearly the leading differences between life in the sixteenth and in the nineteenth centuries, and of the first importance is it to realise how little personal liberty was understood in Elizabethan country towns. Scarcely an entry in the books of the

---

[1] For the general social condition of the reformed municipality, see Mr. Halliwell-Phillipps's invaluable *Life of Shakespeare*, his *New Place* (1864), and his privately printed publication containing the Chamberlain's Accounts 1564-1618, and the Council Books (A and B).

new council fails to emphasise the rigidly paternal character of its rule. If a man lived immorally he was summoned to the guildhall, and rigorously examined as to the truth of the rumours that had reached the bailiff's ear. If his guilt was proved, and he refused to make adequate reparation, he was invited to leave the city. A female servant, hired at a salary of twenty-six shillings and eightpence and a pair of shoes, left her master suddenly in 1611. The aldermen ordered her arrest on her master's complaint. Her defence was that "she was once frightened in the night in the chamber where her master's late wife died, but by what or when she cannot tell"; but this plea proved of no avail, and she spent some months in the gaol by the guildhall. Rude endeavours were made to sweeten the tempers of scolding wives. A substantial "cucking stool," with iron staples, lock, and hinges, was kept in good repair. The shrew was attached to it, and by means of ropes, planks, and wheels, was plunged two or three times into the Avon whenever the municipal council believed her to stand in need of correction. Three days and three nights were invariably spent in the open stocks by any inhabitant who spoke disrespectfully to any town officer, or who disobeyed any minor municipal decree. No one might receive a stranger into his house without the bailiff's permission. No journeyman, apprentice, or servant might "be forth of their or his master's house" after nine o'clock at night. Bowling alleys and butts were provided by the council, but were only to be used at stated times. An alderman was fined on one occasion for going to bowls after a morning meeting of the council, and Henry Sydnall was fined twenty pence for keeping unlawful or unlicensed bowling in a back shed. Alehouse-keepers, of whom there were thirty in Stratford in Shakespeare's time, were kept strictly under the council's control. They were not allowed to brew their own ale, or to encourage tippling, or to serve poor artificers except at stated hours of the day, on pain of fine and imprisonment. Dogs were not to go about the streets unmuzzled. Every inhabitant had to go to church at least once a month, and absentees were liable to penalties of twenty pounds, which in the late years of Elizabeth's reign commissioners came from London to see that the local authorities enforced. Early in the seventeenth century swearing was rigorously prohibited. Laws as to dress were always regularly enforced. In 1577 there were many fines exacted for failure to wear the plain statute woollen caps on Sundays, to which Rosaline makes reference in *Love's Labour's Lost*, and the regulation affected all inhabitants above six years of age. In 1604 "the greatest part" of the population were presented at a great leet, or law-day, "for wearing their apparel contrary to the statute." Nor would it be difficult to quote many other like proofs of the persistent strictness with which the new town council of Stratford, by the enforcement of its own orders and of the statutes of the realm, regulated the inhabitants' whole conduct of life.

X

JOHN SHAKESPEARE IN MUNICIPAL OFFICE AND IN TRADE

It was this sober form of government that demanded William Shakespeare's allegiance from youth to the close of his life, and in his later days there can be no doubt of his loyal conformity to all its precise edicts. It was of this government that his father, John Shakespeare, was an energetic member, filling all the chief offices, from ale-taster and constable to that of bailiff and chief alderman, between 1557 and 1577; and from his boyhood every detail of municipal organisation must have been familiar to the poet.

Before 1557 his father was a leading or "capital" burgess and a member of the town council. He was an ale-taster in 1557, and had to enforce the order "that all the brewers, that

John Shakespeare in Municipal Office

brew to sell either ale or beer, shall sell their ale or beer for threepence the gallon under the hair-sieve (*i.e.* new), and threepence-halfpenny the gallon stale, and thirteen gallons to the dozen, and that no victualler and no alehouse-keeper shall sell any ale or beer contrary to this order; and that all bakers that bake bread to sell shall sell four (*i.e.* quarter) loaves for a penny, two (*i.e.* half) loaves for a penny, and one (*i.e.* whole) loaf for a penny, and so to keep the assize (the testing of weights and measures) delivered every Thursday at night, upon pain of imprisonment." On 30th September 1558, and again on 6th October 1559, John Shakespeare was chosen one of the four constables, and had to direct the watch throughout the year, and, Dogberry-like, once every month, from Michaelmas to Candlemas or oftener, "as the case requireth it, to call to him certain of the council and some other honest men, and keep and have a privy watch for the good rule of the town." In 1559 and in 1561 he was one of the four "affeerors"—officers who assessed in the court-leets fines for minor offences, for which the statutes prescribed no express penalties. From 1561 to 1564 he was a chamberlain, and duly presented year by year the municipal accounts.

On 4th July 1565 John Shakespeare reached the dignity of an alderman. He took the place of William Bott, a wealthy capitalist from Coventry, who relieved William Clopton, an heir of Sir Hugh, of some of his pecuniary difficulties by purchasing New Place of him in 1563. Bott was of a quarrelsome temper. He was evidently one of those self-sufficient blusterers whom William Shakespeare delighted to honour with his ridicule in characters like Bottom and Dogberry. In 1565 Bott brought an action against Richard Sponer, a poor painter, inhabiting a cottage in Chapel Lane, for stealing twelve pieces of squared timber from his garden, and at the same time he had a serious dispute with his fellow-councillors. He spoke evil words of Master Bailiff and others. He said that "there was never an honest man of the council," whereupon he "was sent for and did not come to his answer." On the contrary, he gave "such opprobrious words that he was not," in his fellow-councillors' opinion, "worthy henceforth to be of the council," and was consequently "expulsed, to be none of the company." It was Bott's disgrace that secured John Shakespeare his alderman's gown. Three years later, at Michaelmas 1568, John rose higher and became bailiff, and on 5th September 1571 he was chief alderman, a post which he retained till 3d September of the following year. After Michaelmas 1572 he ceased to take an active part in municipal affairs. The duties of the aldermen could not be well performed by poor men. In 1563 and 1564, when John Shakespeare was chamberlain, he had been able to advance as much as £3 : 2 : 7½ to the corporation, but as the century grew older his monetary resources failed him. In 1564, when the plague raged at Stratford, he had liberally contributed to the funds raised by the aldermen in behalf of their poor and afflicted neighbours. In 1576 he paid twelvepence towards the beadle's salary; but in 1578 he was unable to supply his share of the payments privately made by his fellow-councillors "towards the furniture of three pikemen, two billmen, and one archer," who were apparently sent by the corporation to attend a muster of the trained bands of the county.

Nor was he at the same time able to give the small sum of fourpence for the relief of the poor. Failure to pay such pecuniary dues as these combined, with long-continued absence from the "halls," to cause the corporation, on 6th September 1586, to deprive John Shakespeare of his alderman's gown. He thus retired from public life when his son William was twenty-two years of age, and in no position to give his father any assistance.

John Shakespeare's assumption of municipal office would prove, in the absence of all other evidence, that he was engaged in trade in the town. The first bailiff whose name is recorded was a skinner, and all his successors, with rare exceptions, were business men. When John Shakespeare was first proposed for that office in 1567, the rival candidates were a butcher and a brewer. John Shakespeare's mercantile occupation has been a matter of endless controversy. It is certain that on 17th June 1556 he sued, in the capacity of a glover, before John Burbage, the bailiff, one Thomas Siche, of Arscotte, Worcestershire, for a debt of eight pounds; and between 1565 and 1579, whenever he attached his

John Shakespeare in Municipal Office 109

mark to official documents (he could not write), he rudely drew the glover's trade-mark—an instrument resembling the stretcher still used by sellers of gloves. Twenty-three years later he was always described as a yeoman. But here is no real inconsistency. Stratford still retained many agricultural characteristics. Small farmers lived there in number, and, except those inhabitants exclusively engaged in some recognised urban manufacture, they dealt in all the products yielded by the cultivation of land and stock. Thus, in 1597 George Perry, of Stratford, was described as using, "besides his glover's trade, buying and selling of wool and corn, and making of malt," and Richard Castell, of Rother Market, was a glover, "while his wife uttereth weekly two strikes of malt." Joyce Hobday, a widow, was similarly selling at one time wool, calves' leather, and gloves. John Shakespeare's business was, doubtless, of even wider extent. He cultivated far more land than the majority of his neighbours. About 1557 he married Mary Arden, the youngest daughter of Robert Arden, of Wilmecote, his father's old landlord, and she had inherited from her father "all his land in Wilmecote called Ashbies, and the crop upon the ground, sown and tilled as it is," and was, with her sister Alice, her father's residuary legatee, which gave her arable and pasture land at the little village of Snitterfield. About 1570 John purchased a small farm called Ingon Meadow, containing fourteen acres, for eight pounds. The produce of these estates was, doubtless, sold by John Shakespeare at Stratford. As early as 1556 we find him complaining that his neighbour, Henry Field, unjustly detained barley belonging to him. In 1564 he sold timber to the corporation. Sheep, meat, skins, wool, and leather were among the commodities in which he dealt. That his business transactions were numerous is proved by the frequency of his suits for the recovery of debts in the local courts between 1557 and 1595. His failure after 1580 was probably due to some unfortunate speculation in corn, or to the recurrence of dearths, of which dealers were forbidden by statute law, strictly enforced by the town council, to take any commercial advantage.

XI

THE STRATFORD INDUSTRIES AND POPULATION

DESPITE the absence of strict divisions of trade, and the trading by one person in many distantly-related commodities, John Shakespeare's and his son's contemporaries maintained the trade societies initiated by their mediæval predecessors, and descriptions of the various trading companies are still extant. These societies often embraced the followers of more trades than one, but each society was a very close corporation. "The weaver's art," as in the thirteenth century, held among them the first place. There were, besides, mysteries or crafts of skinners, tailors, shoemakers, saddlers, glovers, whittawers (*i.e.* tanners of white leathers), and collarmakers; a company of chandlers, soapmakers, ironmongers, and bakers, survived beyond 1726. Pewterers butchers, brewers, drapers, grocers, carpenters, and painters were also numerous in the town.

Orders were frequently passed bidding no person set up any trade or occupation "before he be made free of its company," and enjoining on every one the necessity of "sorting himself into one company or another," but almost all the shopkeepers, like John Shakespeare, contrived to follow more than one trade. Thus Adrian Quiney, a prominent mercer, dealt, together with his wife, in such various commodities as ginger, red lead, Southwich cloth, lime, salad oil, and deal boards. This Quiney owned a house in Henley Street, and was bailiff in 1572; his grandson Richard was an intimate friend of the poet, and his great-grandson Thomas married Judith Shakespeare, the poet's younger daughter, just before her father's death in 1616. Shoemaking seems to have formed a more exclusive industry. Among the chief shoemakers of the town was a namesake of John Shakespeare, possibly a cousin, living in 1590 in Bridge Street. He filled municipal office as constable and ale-taster in 1585, and was master of the company of shoemakers in

The Stratford Industries and Population

1585. In 1587 he was in pecuniary difficulties, and received a loan of five pounds from the corporation out of Oken's Charity—a fund bequeathed to the town by Thomas Oken, of Warwick, in 1570, for the relief of poor tradesmen. Soon afterwards he appears to have left Stratford.

Certain regulations like those enforced upon bakers and brewers by the ale-tasters, or those enforced by the tannery searchers, hampered, with advantage to the consumer, the freedom of trade. There were customs of stretching and straining cloths, and of chalking and "otherwise deceitfully making them," which were frequently prohibited under rigorous penalties. Leather was often imperfectly tanned and made hollow by divers mixtures, such as obnoxious fats, so that "boots within two or three days' wearing will straightway become brown as a hare-back; and, which is more, fleet and run about like a dishclout; and which is most of all, hold out no water or very little." Horse-hide was often sold for ox-hide. Corn dealers were ordered, under heavy penalties, in 1596, not to "ingross, forestall, or regrate," but "to furnish the market rateably and weekly" with fixed quantities. These prohibitions often affected traders disastrously, but their customers invariably benefited.

Trade was maintained at a normal rate of briskness by the weekly markets and the half-yearly fairs, the chief of which fell in September. The town council strictly regulated the procedure of the fairs, and appointed to each trade a station in the streets. Thus, raw hides at markets and fairs were to be laid down at the cross in Rother Market. Sellers of butter, cheese, all manner of white meat, wick-yarn, and fruits were to set up their stalls by the cross at the chapel. A site in the High Street was assigned to country butchers, who repaired to the town with their flesh, hides, and tallow. Pewterers were ordered to "pitch" their wares in Wood Street, and to pay for the ground they occupied fourpence a yard. Saltwains, whose owners did a thriving trade in days when salted meats formed the staple supply of food, were permitted to stand about the cross in Rother Market. At various points the victuallers were permitted to erect booths. These regulations were needful to prevent strife, and fines for breach of the rules often

The Stratford Industries and Population

reached as large a sum as five pounds. The townsmen were anxious to secure for themselves all the advantages of these gatherings, and the council often employed men armed with cudgels to keep Coventry traders out of the town.

These details, which are drawn from the council books of the Stratford Corporation from 1557 to 1607, indicate much commercial activity. For a country town, we may judge Stratford to have been fairly populous. We know that the commissioners appointed to report on the guild in 1547 stated the chapel to be the chief place of worship for fifteen hundred "houseling people," *i.e.* persons accustomed to take the holy sacrament. In 1562 there appeared to have been about thirty householders in each of the twelve streets of the town, which would roughly show a population of two thousand persons. Plagues, like the disastrous one of 1564, were continually reducing the population, but new arrivals from the neighbouring villages appear to have maintained it at a fairly steady average. Small farmers were finding agriculture growing year by year less profitable; the great city merchants had long been buying up arable-land to transform it into pasture-land, sheep and wool were now more profitable commodities than wheat or barley or oats, and the new landlords only cultivated their estates with a view to securing the largest profits. Far less labour was required in tending sheep than in growing corn. Agricultural labourers, therefore, found their services at a discount, and flocked to the towns. The yeomen too found it to their advantage to move into towns, where their produce could readily find purchasers. Stratford, we have seen, attracted a rich man like William Bott from Coventry, about 1560. Some years before it had attracted from the neighbouring village of Snitterfield John Shakespeare himself.

XII

JOHN SHAKESPEARE'S FIRST SETTLEMENT IN
STRATFORD—THE STREETS

IT was, in all probability, in 1551, just before the borough had reached the all-important stage of incorporation, that John Shakespeare first came to Stratford. In the Middle Ages there were no Shakespeares at Stratford. But in the surrounding districts families of the name were numerous. Thus, among the members of a guild—which closely resembled the Stratford guild—at Knoll, near Hampton-in-Arden, Shakespeares, Shaxpers, Shakespeyres, Shakspeeres, called Richard, John, William, Agnes, Isabella, are found repeatedly between 1464 and 1555. Some of these lived at Rowington, and can be traced there till the close of the last century; one Thomas Shakespeare, of Rowington, was a disciple of Jack Cade. A family of

Shakespeares also lived at Warwick till the close of the sixteenth century, and on 16th June 1579 William, one of these, according to the register in the church of St. Nicholas, Warwick, met his death by drowning in the river

SHAKESPEARE'S BIRTHPLACE BEFORE RESTORATION.

Avon. (How invaluable might this piece of evidence prove to the monomaniacs who believe that Bacon wrote Will Shakespeare's plays!)

But the poet, although doubtless collaterally related to many of these families, was directly descended from none of them. John Shakespeare probably belonged to a branch residing in the sixteenth century at Snitterfield, a little village four miles to the north of Stratford, and the Richard Shakespeare who was a farmer, renting there of Robert Arden of Wilmecote a small tenement, with a little land attached to it, in 1550, was doubtless John's father and the poet's grandfather.

Snitfield, or Snitterfield, had seen days of commercial prosperity, but it was at this time chiefly occupied by small farmers and their labourers. It had a church at the time of the Norman Conquest, and in 1242 a market and a fair had been granted it. As a manor it had successively belonged to a monastery of Bordsley and to many Earls of Warwick, and it came, in the sixteenth century, into the hands of John Hales, the founder of a free school at Coventry—a very wealthy man, whose lameness, the result of an accident, gained for him the sobriquet of "Hales with the club foot." In 1552 John Shakespeare was living in Henley Street, Stratford, but it was not until 1556 that he purchased houses in the town. In that year he entered into copyhold possession of two tenements, one with a garden and croft (*i.e.* an enclosed plot of land), in Greenhill Street, at a rental of sixpence, and another with a garden only in Henley Street. But these dwellings he apparently let again, and continued to reside in the house he had first occupied in Henley Street. This tenement he bought, with its gardens, orchards, and the house adjoining, which had been previously in his occupation for business purposes, for forty pounds, in 1575. It was in an upper story of the former of these houses that his son William was born in 1564, probably on 23d April. It is of interest to note that the nearest neighbours of John Shakespeare were on one side John Wheler, and on the other, before 1591, George Badger, a draper, who was once constable of the town. It was, doubtless, among their children that William Shakespeare found his earliest playfellows.

It may be well to follow John Shakespeare from his first entrance into the town, and take a survey of it in his company. We shall thus gain some knowledge of that aspect of it with which his son William was familiar in his youth. John Shakespeare would have originally entered Stratford by the Warwick Road, near which Snitterfield lies, and would have found himself on arrival at the bottom of Bridge Street, by

SNITTERFIELD CHURCH.

the causeway leading to the stone bridge. Leland, the antiquarian traveller of 1530, said of the general appearance presented by Stratford to a stranger, " It hath two or three long streets, besides back lanes. One of the principal streets leadeth from east to west, and another from north to south. . . . The town is reasonable well builded of timber." Passing up Bridge Street, which led on from east to west, the new-comer came upon a small row of shops and stalls in the centre of the road known as Middle Row, of which the south side was Bridge Street, and the north, Back Bridge Street. It was in Bridge Street, it will be remembered, that John Shakespeare, the shoemaker, had his stall. The row was pulled down less than a century ago to form the wide thoroughfare of modern Bridge Street. In Bridge Street stood the three chief inns of the town—the Swan, the Bear, and the Crown, of which the latter is believed to have occupied the site of the present Red Horse Hotel; and for many years a large house there, known as the Cage, and probably at one time the prison, was in the occupation of Henry Smith, a vintner. When the top of Bridge Street was reached, it divided into two roads—Wood Street to the left and Henley Street to the right—and the latter soon led into the country. Wood Street ran on into Greenhill Street, afterwards Moor Town's End, which, though still retaining a rural hedge, was fringed with a few houses. Behind Henley Street lay gravel-pits belonging to the guild, which were largely used in the repair of the bridge, and in rare paving operations in the town; but no inhabitant was allowed to help himself there. At right angles to the west end of Wood Street was Rother Market, where a stone cross stood, and the borough's weekly cattle market was held, and thence lanes led to Evesham.

The chief or market cross of the town was at the head, *i.e.* the west end of Bridge Street, at the corner of High Street, which ran parallel to Rother Market. It was a stone monument covered by a low tiled shed, round which forms were placed for the accommodation of listeners to the sermons, which, as at St. Paul's Cross, London, were occasionally delivered there. At a later date a room was placed above it, and a clock above that. The open space about it formed the chief market-place of the town, and

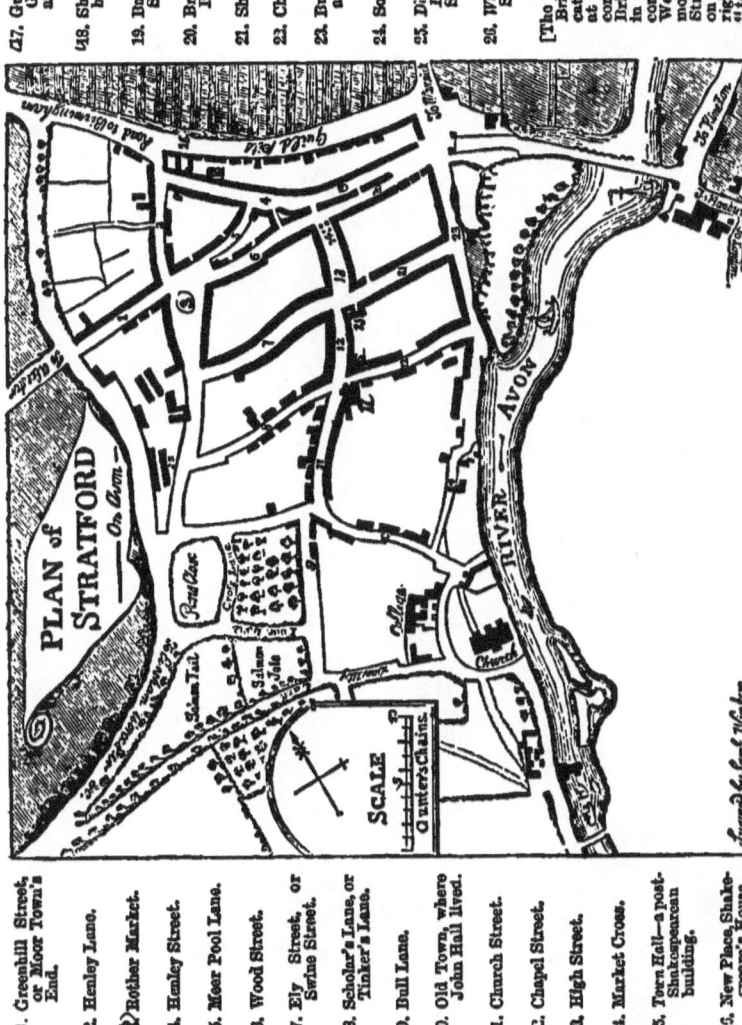

1. Greenhill Street, or Moor Town's End.
2. Henley Lane.
3. Rother Market.
4. Henley Street.
5. Meer Pool Lane.
6. Wood Street.
7. Ely Street, or Swine Street.
8. Scholar's Lane, or Tinker's Lane.
9. Bull Lane.
10. Old Town, where John Hall lived.
11. Church Street.
12. Chapel Street.
13. High Street.
14. Market Cross.
15. Town Hall—a post-Shakespearean building.
16. New Place, Shakespeare's House.
17. Guild Chapel, Grammar School and Guild Hall.
18. Shakespeare's birth-place.
19. Back Bridge Street.
20. Bridge, or Fore Bridge Street.
21. Sheep Street.
22. Chapel Lane.
23. Buildings known as Waterside.
24. Southam's Lane.
25. Dissenters' Meeting House (post-Shakespearean.)
26. White Lion (post-Shakespearean).

[The Mill and Mill Bridge are indicated on the river at the left-hand corner of the map. Dodgo Town lies in the right-hand corner. The Great Western Railway's modern station at Stratford is built on ground to the right of the road "to Alcester."]

GROUND PLAN OF STRATFORD-ON-AVON, MADE IN 1759, AND INDICATING ALL THE FEATURES FAMILIAR TO SHAKESPEARE.

(Reproduced by kind permission of the late Mr. J. O. Halliwell-Phillipps from his History of New Place.

its site is now occupied by a house known as the Market-house. At the pump which stood near it housewives were frequently to be seen "washing of clothes," and hanging them up on the cross to dry, or the butchers might be detected hanging meat there; but these practices were disapproved of by the corporation, and finally forbidden in 1608. The stocks, pillory, and whipping-post were set up hard by the cross.

From the high or market cross, the street that ran in a south-westerly direction introduced the visitor to the most substantial buildings of the town, and from the householders there the bailiff was usually chosen. In other parts of Stratford most of the houses were detached; here there were a few vacant spaces, but the houses mostly adjoined each other. The first portion was the High Street, and mainly consisted of shops. The second portion was Chapel Street, and among the large private houses there stood New Place, which in 1597 became William Shakespeare's property. The lower end of the street was known as Church Street, and at the corner, facing New Place, was the chapel of the guild, succeeded by the school, guildhall, gaol, and almshouses. Above the chapel-porch was a third cross, and near at hand a second pump, which was removed by the council's order in 1595, and its site filled with gravel and rubbish. Turning to the left at the end of the street, Old Town was reached, where gardens and unoccupied land surrounded several large houses. John Hall, one of the poet's sons-in-law, had a residence there early in the seventeenth century. This road ultimately led to the churchyard and to the parish church, by the banks of the river, "a fair large piece of work," as Leland describes it, ". . . at the south end of the town." Over against the church was a stately residence of the Combes, formerly the College of Stratford, and but a little way down the road that ran between its grounds and the cemetery were the river-mill and the mill-bridge, which was not pulled down till late in the present century. By the river, near the church, doubtless stood the cucking-stool for the scolding wives, and a field belonging to the town in the neighbourhood was known as the bank-croft, or bancroft, where drovers and farmers of the town were allowed to take their cattle to pasture for an hour a day. "All horses, geldings, mares, swine, geese, ducks, and other cattle" found there contrary to this regulation were impounded by the beadle in the pinfold, which was situated near at hand.

The back lanes of which Leland wrote stretched from Rother Market to the river, and intersected High Street and its continuations. The chief of them was Ely Street, or Swine Street, joining High Street at its junction with Chapel Street, and running to the Avon as Sheep, or Ship, Street. Parallel with these roads were Scholar's Lane, or Tinker's Lane, crossing Chapel Street by New Place, and thence to the river bearing the name of Chapel Lane, or Dead Lane, or Walker Street. In both Tinker's and Chapel Lanes were gravel-pits, digging in which was strictly fordidden within eight feet of the road. Many cottages in the smaller thoroughfares did service as alehouses.

XIII

THE CONSTRUCTION AND FURNITURE OF THE HOUSES—THE GARDENS

THE visitor to modern Stratford will learn from this account of the streets of the town in the sixteenth century how kindly time has dealt with their names. Nor of the outward appearances of the houses in Shakespeare's day will his own observation fail to give him a good conception. The majority of them, two stories high, were constructed of timber beams, set crosswise far apart, with the panels or interstices of lath and plaster. The roofs were usually of thatch, with dormer windows nestling there when the front wall did not rise into steep gables. Porches shaded the door; often a narrow, slanting, tiled or wooden roof ran along the house front over the window on the ground floor, and beneath this kind of shed,

THE RED HORSE HOTEL.

called a pentice or penthouse, the smaller traders set a stall for their goods. The better houses in High Street and Chapel Street, like New Place, were of timber and brick, instead of plaster, and Shakespeare appears to have rebuilt the greater part of his residence with stone, of which the College was wholly constructed. Tiled roofs were characteristic of such buildings, but at times an owner of conservative tendencies would insist on the superiority of thatch, like Walter Roche, who moved into a house in Chapel Street in 1582, and replaced the tiles with thatch. Occasionally the woodwork in the front of the houses, as in the surviving example in High Street, built in 1596, was carefully carved with *fleurs de lis* and interlacing designs, and the oriel windows and overhanging beams were supported by carved brackets. Chapel Lane, one of the streets well within the town, and others in its outlying districts, like the rural parts of Henley and Greenhill Streets, were chiefly occupied by barns, where the grain from the neighbouring country, largely cultivated by the townsmen, was stored. These were constructed like the smaller dwelling-houses — of timber, lath, and plaster, and were invariably thatched.

The gardens of the houses were separated from each other by mud walls, which were constructed of clay, road-sand, or mud, and usually thatched at the top. In constant need of repair, they afforded little protection against robbers, who often forced their way through them. The land about the houses was very generally planted with fruit-trees, and the orchard about the guild buildings was noted for its plums and apples. The garden of New Place was long famed for its mulberries. Pleasure gardens were an exclusive characteristic of the great manor-houses in the surrounding country, but it is certain that flowers and a few cooking and medicinal plants were cultivated in the small plots in the town, and it is quite possible that more ambitious attempts at horticulture were made in the exceptionally large gardens of New Place and the College. Elm-trees were a very common feature of the Stratford gardens. In 1582 it was reported to the council that of four backyards in Dead or Chapel Lane—the street where the barns predominated—there were eleven elms and one ash-tree growing in one of them, twenty-six elms in another, one in the third, and four in the fourth. Several gardens in Henley Street could boast of at least four elms, and elm-trees marking the borough's boundaries on the Birmingham and Evesham roads were surveyed with much ceremony in Rogation Week year after year by the town officers. Thus the town was well shaded in summer, and he who would learn the rudiments of forestry had little need to go far afield. Shakespeare frequently indicates a significant familiarity with the pruning of trees and the simpler operations of horticulture. His gardener in *Richard II* has no dilettante acquaintance with the method of cutting off "the heads of too fast-growing sprays," or of rooting away

> The noisome weeds, that without profit suck
> The soil's fertility from wholesome flowers.

At the proper season he wounds

> The bark, the skin of our fruit-trees;
> Lest, being over-proud with sap and blood,
> With too much riches it confound itself.

Others of Shakespeare's characters give very adequate explanation of the gardener's hatred of weeds, of " hateful dock, rough thistles, kexies, burs," of "tooth'd briars, sharp furzes, pricking gorse and thorns"; they well knew the evil work wrought by "envious worms and caterpillars," and were not ignorant of the uses of manure for those roots

> That shall first spring and be most delicate.

Iago's specious philosophy finds its most vigorous expression in his comparison of "our bodies" to "our gardens, to the which our wills are gardeners," where we may "plant nettles or sow lettuce; set hyssop and weed up thyme; supply it with one gender of herbs or distract it with many." This practical knowledge was doubtless acquired while the poet was working with his father in the garden or orchard about his home in Henley Street, and was developed later in the "great garden" about his own residence in Chapel Street.

The interior of the Elizabethan houses of Stratford had little of what we understand by comfort. In the smaller houses for a long period chimneys were rare. A mere hole in the wall allowed the smoke to escape. In many cases the internal space was not partitioned off. The ground floor formed a single

THE ROOM IN WHICH SHAKESPEARE WAS BORN.

"hall," and "each one made his fire against a reredos in the hall, where he dined and dressed his meat." In the case of the larger houses, the hall was likewise the chief apartment, and a single loft above, sometimes divided, formed the only sleeping-room, but here there was usually a parlour and another chamber cut off from the hall and cellars and outhouses devoted to the buttery. A change for the better came over Stratford in the matter of chimneys towards the close of the century. They were added to many of the little tenements of Middle Row, and John Shakespeare's house in Henley Street could certainly boast of one of them. A chimney was constructed for the kitchen at the guild chambers, and in 1582 an order was passed by the town council that "Walter Hill, dwelling in Rother Market, and all the other inhabitants of the borough, shall, before St. James's Day, 30th April, make sufficient chimneys," under pain of a fine of ten shillings. To the absence of chimneys the continual recurrence of severe fires at Stratford in the sixteenth century was mainly due.

Of the furniture of such a house as that in which the poet was born in Henley Street, we obtain an adequate account from an inventory made in 1592, on the death of Henry Field, tanner, a near neighbour of John Shakespeare. John Shakespeare was his chief executor. In the hall there was "one table upon a joined frame, five small joint stools, a small chair, a wainscot bench, and painted cloths," *i.e.* hangings of cloth or canvas painted in oil. There was evidently a stove there, doubtless the only one in the house, for andirons, fire shovel, tongs, pothooks, and pothangers are among the furnishings. In the parlour, the sitting-room by day and bedroom apparently by night, was a small table upon a frame, two joint stools, two chairs, a press, a joined bed, and a small plank. "Item, three painted cloths, one feather bed, one flock bed, two bolsters, one pillow, one bed covering of yellow and green, four old blankets, and one old carpet." A long chest in the room contained coarse sheets, coarse table cloths, coarse wipers (*i.e.* dusters), and table napkins. In a shorter coffer were three pairs of flaxen sheets, one pair of hempen sheets, one flaxen table cloth, another of hemp, half a dozen table napkins of flax and one of hemp, two diaper napkins,

THE UPPER STORY OF SHAKESPEARE'S BIRTHPLACE.

and four pillow-cases of flax. In the buttery were dishes, pewter platters, saucers, porridge dishes, salt cellars, candlesticks, a quart pot, a pint pot, and two flower pots. Of brass there were three pots, a little pan, six skimmers, a basin, one chaffing dish, a frying pan, and a dripping pan. There were also in the buttery four spits, great and small, and a pair of cupboards. In the chamber next the parlour were a truckle bed which could be rolled up by day, an old coverlet, an old bolster, an old blanket, a little round table, and two old chests. In a little room adjoining were more beds, coffers, and a press of boards with shelves. In the kitchen house were six barrels of beer, five looms, four pails, four forms, three stools, one bolting hutch, two "skips" for taking up yeast, one vat, a table board, two pairs of trestles, and two strikes (*i.e.* bushel measures), besides an axe, shovels, and spade. In an upper chamber were more beds and bedding, a cheese-crate, malt, malt shovels, a beam with scales, two dozen trenchers, and one dozen pewter spoons. In the yard were bundles of laths, loads of wood, buckets, cord and windlass for the well, and a watchman's bill.

Another house, the property of a wooldriver, of which John Shakespeare also made an inventory, contained a similar array of tables, chairs, beds, bedding, painted cloths, and brass and pewter implements. There were also three green cushions for a window seat, a curtain for the window, and pots of earth and glass. The presence of brewing utensils and looms in both instances show that it was customary to brew ale and weave wool at home. But what gaps suggest themselves in these inventories to the modern reader! Henry Field's wealth of table napkins, which were used freely after the meal was done, emphasise the total absence of knives and forks. Jugs, basins, and towels are conspicuously rare.

It is noticeable, too, how the furnitures of the sleeping-rooms and sitting-rooms encroached upon one another, and how gradually the modern distinction grew up. The cooking was chiefly done in the hall, upon which the front door opened; and there the pothooks and hangers were always kept. The tables, as a rule, were made with flaps, to "turn up." Capulet, when he wants room for the dancers in his hall, shouts out to his servants to " turn the tables up." The painted cloths, or arras, were features prominent in all Elizabethan houses, whether rich or poor. They were nailed on the walls of the guildhall, and even in the smaller cottages they were met with, bearing in in all cases " wise sayings painted upon them," and frequently rough representations of Bible stories, especially of Dives and Lazarus and of " the pamper'd Prodigal." Shakespeare writes of these hangings in " Lucrece "—

> Who fears a sentence, or an old man's saw,
> Shall by a painted cloth be kept in awe.

Orlando taunts Jaques with having studied his cynical questions from "right painted cloth." Despite the scantiness of bedroom furniture, there was some attempt at decoration. The bed coverings, or counterpanes—there was one of yellow and green belonging to Henry Field —were often richly embroidered, like those in Gremio's city house. The carpet owned by Henry Field was doubtless to cover the table, not to lie beneath it. Grumio, Petruchio's servant, sees "the carpets laid" for supper on the return home of his master and new mistress. The floors were strewn with rushes, or occasionally with sweet-smelling herbs. A Dutch physician, visiting London in 1560, notes how "the chambers and parlours strewn over with sweet herbs refreshed me." Grumio bids the rushes be strewn in Petruchio's house; and Romeo bids wantons, light of heart,

> Tickle the senseless rushes with their heels.

Shakespeare, like his own Gremio, clearly took careful notice of the

> Pewter and brass, and all things that belong
> To house, or housekeeping.

THE BIRTHPLACE OF SHAKESPEARE.

I.

XIV

THE SANITARY CONDITION OF THE TOWN

SANITARY arrangements within the house were obviously not much heeded. The clay floors, whether or no strewn with rushes, attracted all manner of refuse, and were rarely swept. The well in the garden and the town pump might have formed an adequate water supply; but the uses of water were not generally known. The mud walls between the gardens were not conducive to cleanliness. Very few of the ordinary laws of health were, in fact, observed by the householders; and the corporation made very feeble attempts to enforce such of them as, when neglected, created very obvious nuisances. Frequent penalties were imposed on those who failed to scour and clean the gutters and ditches before their residences. But the difficulty of disposing of household refuse was very commonly met by "laying it in the streets and lanes," or in these ditches and gutters. John Shakespeare appears to have been an habitual offender in this respect. His name first appears in any record of the municipality as owing a fine of twelvepence for having made a dirt heap with his neighbours Adrian Quiney and Henry Reynolds in Henley Street. Six years later he "stood amerced" in fourpence for failing to keep his gutter clean. In 1563, and subsequent years, the exposure of domestic rubbish in the street rendered the offender liable to a forfeit of three shillings and fourpence, and "the tenant that renteth the ground" upon which the "muckhill" stood, to one of ten shillings. Six places in the town were appointed for the amassing of the filth in legalised "muckhills." One stood in Ship Street, another in Scholar's Lane, a third in Henley Street, but the chief was in Chapel Lane. They were, in almost all cases, at the rural end of the smaller streets; but as they were to be removed only "twice a year—that is to say, before the feast of Pentecost, and near about Michaelmas," they were sufficiently near to human habitations to make them a constant source of danger

OLD HOUSES IN ROTHER STREET.

The Sanitary Condition of the Town

to health and life. Butchers, it is true, were forbidden to use them, and were ordered, under a penalty of twenty shillings, to take their garbage out of the town at nine o'clock each evening.

Chapel Lane, which ran by the side of New Place, was the filthiest part of the town. The small cottagers there habitually neglected the council's orders, and dispersed refuse in the open road, until it often became impassable. John Sadler, a miller, insisted on winnowing his peas there, and leaving the chaff about. But this was a very innocent offence. Most of his neighbours kept pigs, who, in spite of repeatedly published prohibitions, were allowed to wander at their own sweet wills. If a pigs-cote or pigsty was built, it was on the lane's pathway, and fines could not break the house-holders of the practice. John Rogers, the vicar of Stratford, living by the guild chapel, in 1613 was remonstrated with by the council for an offence of this kind, and his irrelevant defence was to the effect that "about my house there is no place of convenience without much annoyance to the chapel," which was next door, and "how far," he proceeded, "the breeding of such creatures is needful to poor housekeepers, I refer myself to those that can equal my charge," *i.e.* have as many expenses as I. The town council issued an order in 1611 "that no swine be permitted to be in the open street of this town unless they have a keeper with them, and then only while they are in driving within this borough, upon pain for every strayer of fourpence." But this produced little effect. Every time Shakespeare left his house in New Place (for the doorway was in Chapel Lane), he crossed the most noisome thoroughfare in the town; and Mr. Halliwell-Phillipps's suggestion that his death in 1616, like that of many of his townsmen, was due to the tainted atmosphere of his environment, seems only too probable. And Stratford saw no rapid improvement in the matter. Garrick described the town in 1769 as "the most dirty, unseemly, ill-pav'd, wretched-looking town in all Britain."

Paternal as was the tone of the town council's edicts, it never supplemented the householder's neglect of cleanliness by any really adequate provisions. It delegated the duty of keeping the streets clean to the townsfolk, and as they failed to perform this function the streets re-

The Sanitary Condition of the Town

mained dirty. It alone undertook the cleansing of the bridge, the market-place, and the space before the chapel door and guildhall; but in these days of the glorification of hygiene there is a ludicrous ring about all the details of the arrangements made for this object. For the sweeping of the market-place, in Shakespeare's day, a widow named Baker was employed at a yearly salary of six shillings and eightpence, and she was provided, at the municipal expense, with a shovel, a broomstick, and twigs of trees. The duty of sweeping the bridge was entrusted to a man named Raven, who at times secured the additional services of the widow Baker. The chapel was rarely defiled by water; but on the occasion of the repair of its roof in 1604, Anthony Rees and his wife with goodwife Wilson were directed to sweep away the cobwebs and to wash the seats. Fresh rushes were occasionally laid in the council chamber and guildhall; and the floor of the latter was renewed at intervals with clay.

There was little pavement about the town. The market-place, in fact, alone was paved. But the bridge and the causeway were kept in fair order by the liberal sprinkling of gravel from the guild pits. In other parts of the town "logs and blocks" lay about the roadways, "to the nuisance of the king's liege people." Arrangements were made for a short time in winter for the lighting of the town. In 1557 it was ordained that every alderman and "capital" burgess, "between 15th December and twenty days after Christmas, from five to eight o'clock in the evening, have a lanthorn hanging in the street before his door, and there a candle burning to give light," under pain to forfeit twelvepence in default. In 1617 the dates ran from 1st November to 2d February.

XV

PLAGUES, FIRES, FLOODS, AND FAMINES

THE whole town had to pay heavy penalties of disease for its indifference to sanitary precautions. The plague, a scourge of Christendom, whose horrors are barely paralleled by the fatal progresses now made from time to time in Europe by the Asiatic cholera, paid Stratford repeated visits. Few decades passed without its appearance among the townspeople. The infection rapidly passed from house to house, with its burning fevers and icy shiverings, its cureless pains and fatal languors. No remedy was known to produce much effect on the course of the disease. Bleedings and draughts of the plague-water were of no avail. Sorrel-water and verjuice, with oranges and lemons, allayed for a time the patient's thirst, and he was advised to take often, and in small quantities, light food like rabbit or chicken.

Cleanliness was enjoined, with rare success, to prevent the spread of the contagion. Windows were to be kept open, and hung with green boughs of oak and willow; the floors to be strewn with sorrel, lettuce, roses, and oak-leaves, or with vinegar and rose-water; sandal-wood and musk, aloes, amber, and cinnamon were to burn about the houses six hours a day. The lighting of fires of rosemary and bay was the sole precaution habitually taken in small cottages at these troublous times (see Froude's *History*, vol. vii. pp. 74, 75).

The claims of death rarely remained unsatisfied: high and low fell before the pestilence; and graves in the churchyards stood always open to receive new dwellers, as soon as they had yielded their last breath. The most fearful epidemic that Stratford knew came in the summer of 1564, when William Shakespeare was two or three months old. One-seventh of the inhabitants of Stratford was swept away and consigned to the cemetery on the banks of the Avon. John Shakespeare's house was happily spared, and he did his duty

THE HOUSE OF DR. JOHN HALL.

to his poor neighbours. The town council feared to meet in their chamber, but frequently assembled in the garden adjoining to discuss measures for the relief of the poor. Many twelvepences John Shakespeare and his fellow-councillors bestowed on "those that be visited" between August and October of the fatal year.

Of the terrors of the day one tradition preserves a vivid picture. Clopton manor-house was attacked. Charlotte Clopton, a young girl of the family, whose portrait shows fair blue eyes and pale golden hair falling in wavy ringlets on her neck, sickened of the disease, and, to all appearance, died. The body was hurried into the family tomb beneath Stratford church. Before a week had passed another of the house followed her, and was borne to the same vault. And there the bearers saw by their torches, on the steps leading from the church to the sepulchral chamber, Charlotte Clopton, in her grave-clothes, leaning against the wall. She was dead then, but it was clear that the plague had spared her: after she had been laid in the gloomy vault there had been a terrible struggle for life. Juliet's fears had a very real justification. Charlotte Clopton had been stifled in the vault,

> To whose foul mouth no healthsome air breathes in,
> And there died strangled ere [assistance] came.

Perhaps she had awoke

> Early—what with loathsome smells,
> And shrieks like mandrakes torn out of the earth,
> That living mortals, hearing them, run mad:

and had, as Juliet foretold, become distraught,

> Environed with all these hideous fears.

Fire was another danger to life and property with which the municipal council failed to deal adequately. Towards the close of the century, in 1598, two severe fires visited the town, and so many houses were reported to be "decayed with fire," that a special exemption from the national subsidies was granted the inhabitants. Barns seemed to have suffered repeatedly. The council, by its order of 1582, bidding all householders to erect chimneys for their houses, attempted to stem the fiery tide. They purchased five hooks as early as 1576 for pulling down threatened buildings, and one seems to have always been hung at the entrance to the guildhall. A wise precaution was contained in an edict enjoining on every burgess the necessity of having one leathern bucket, to be

Plagues, Fires, Floods, and Famines

used in case of fire, and on every alderman that of having two. But, none the less, the town continued to suffer, and parts of Henley Street seem often to have been aflame.

A third danger to Stratford was less preventible. The Avon, as it still continues to do, often flooded its banks, and it did no little injury from time to time to the bridge. Stone to fill a hole in the bridge was a frequent item of expenditure in the town's accounts. In 1598 William Shakespeare, probably engaged in restoring New Place, sold for that purpose one load of stone to the corporation for tenpence. A very disastrous flood visited Stratford in 1588, and in the parish register of the neighbouring village of Welford a picturesque account may be found of its coming.

On the 18th day of July 1588 (runs the register), in the morning, there happened about eight of the clock, in Avon, such a sudden flood, as carried away all the hay about Avon. Old Father Porter, buried about four years past, being then a hundred and nine years of age, never knew it so high by a yard and a half. Dwelling in the mill-house, he, in former times, knew it under his bed, but this flood was a yard and a half in the house, and came in so suddenly that John Perry's wife was so amazed that she sate still till she was almost drowned, and was wellnigh beside herself, and so far amiss that she did not know her own child when it was brought in to her. It brake down Grange Mill; the crack thereof was heard at Holditch. It brake up sundry houses in Warwick town, and carried away their bread, beef, cheese, butter, pots, pans, and provisions, and took away ten carts out of one town, and three wains, with the furniture of Mr. Thomas Lucy, and broke both ends of Stratford Bridge. That [flood] drowned three furlongs of corn in Thetford field. It was so high at the height that it unthatched the mill, and stocked up a number of willows and sallows, and did take away one [of] Sales's daughters of Grafton, out of Hillborough meadow, removing of the hay-cock, that she had no shift but to get upon the top of a hay-cock, and was carried thereupon by the water a quarter of a mile wellnigh, till she came to the very last bank of the stream, and there was taken into a boat, and all was like to be drowned, but that another boat coming rescued them soon. Three men going over Stratford Bridge, when they came to the middle of the bridge they could not go forward, and then returning presently, could not get back, for the water was so risen; it rose a yard every hour from eight to four, that it came into the parsonage of Welford Orchard, and filled the fish-pool, and took away the sign-post at the Bear; it carried away Edward Butler's cart, which was soon beneath Bidford, and it came into the vicarage of Weston, and made Adam Sandars thence remove, and took away half a hundred pounds of hay.

So quaint a list of disasters well illustrates Shakespeare's own account, in *Midsummer Night's Dream*, of how the winds—

>Falling in the land,
Have every pelting river made so proud,

OLD LYCH-GATE AT WELFORD.

> That they have overborne their continents :
> The ox hath therefore stretched his yoke in vain,
> The ploughman lost his sweat; and the green corn
> Hath rotted, ere his youth attained a beard. . . .

It was doubtless at Stratford, too, that Shakespeare learnt how in such seasons " the moon, the governess of floods, . . . washes all the air,

> That rheumatic diseases do abound.

Besides the dangers of plagues, fires, and floods, Stratford ran sometimes the risk of starvation. Grain at times was so scarce that the corporation had to distribute corn on its own account, and made an inventory of all to be found in the town. One of the most serious dearths occurred in 1598, and "the note of corn and malt taken" at the time is extant. John Shakespeare appears to have owned none, but his son, at New Place, had as much as ten quarters, a quantity which few of his neighbours exceeded. The laws enforced against grain-dealers, prohibiting them from buying up corn to sell at famine prices in times of dearth, broke undoubtedly the violence of these visitations, but they did not come without forcing many to suffer.

These details will help us to form a good working conception of the conditions of business life led by Shakespeare's father, and by the majority of the poet's contemporaries and fellow-townsmen. We can picture John Shakespeare of a morning wrapping his gown about him, and cursing the pigs that impede his progress, as he hurries past the market-cross down High Street, when the clock strikes nine, on his way to a meeting of the town council in the guildhall or council chamber, We can watch him on a market day purchasing pewter ware in Wood Street or salt in Rother Market, and at the fair driving a brisk trade on his own account in wool, corn, and gloves. Now and then, by means of tallies, he reckons up his gains and losses, and laments the slackness of trade and the perversity of debtors and creditors. He takes an intelligent interest in his garden and orchard, and sees the apples stored in autumn. He visits his namesake in Bridge Street when he is in need of boots, and is on intimate terms with Richard Sponer, the painter, of Chapel Lane, who has been persecuted by the town bully, William Bott. Every night in winter he carefully hangs a lamp out before his house, and before nine o'clock he and his household are at rest. Sometimes he is summoned later by cries of fire, and has to work his two buckets in behalf of a neighbour's barn or house. He cannot write nor read, but he has a distant respect for book-learning. Nothing indeed that he does or has done, amid his serious and prosaic avocations, seems likely to invest his children with anything akin to the genius of poetry. Nevertheless, while he is still striving with declining success to make a living out of the wool and gloves that he keeps stored in his house in Henley Street, it is his eldest son who becomes the brightest of all lights in the firmament of English poetry.

XVI

DOMESTIC AND SCHOOL DISCIPLINE

A STRICT discipline, similar in principle to that enforced by the town council upon the burgesses, was maintained by the sober citizens within their own dwellings over their servants and children. From his earliest infancy we can roughly trace the stern habits of life in which attempts were made to train William Shakespeare. The "Books of Nurture" frequently published in the sixteenth century illustrate the manners which the middle-class father strove to impress upon his sons. The boy was to rise at six o'clock in the morning, carefully to attend to the more necessary portions of his toilet, and to brush his clothes. At meals he had to lay the table and wait on his parents, in whose presence he was not to talk or laugh but in moderation. After his

An old Ale-house. Stratford on Avon.

Domestic and School Discipline 171

parents rose from the table, he might say his grace and take his own meal. His modes of eating and drinking were carefully regulated. In the streets he had to take off his cap to his elders. He was to go to bed early, and say prayers morning and evening. The father was not to be sparing in the use of the rod.

John Shakespeare and his wife Mary Arden, who was related to a good county family, and, perhaps, was herself well educated, were evidently determined to give their eldest son as good an education as Stratford afforded. Doubtless the clerk of the town, like the clerk of Chatham in 2 *Henry VI*, who is detected by Cade's followers "setting of boys' copies," was capable of teaching the boys the hornbook—such writing and reading as enabled them to gain admission to the grammar school. It was probably about 1571 that William proceeded for the first time to the schoolhouse.

The dissolution of the Stratford guild did not involve, as we have seen, the dissolution of the old school of the guild. On the margin of the report made by the King's Commissioners in 1548 a royal officer wrote,

"Continuetur schola quousque," and the school entered soon afterwards on a new lease of life. In June 1553 it was created by royal charter, "The King's New School of Stratford-upon-Avon"—"a certain free grammar school, to consist of one master and teacher, hereafter for ever to endure." The schoolmaster was to be appointed by the Earl of Warwick, to whom the manor and borough had been granted when the Bishop of Worcester's claim was ignored, and he was to receive twenty pounds a year, which was to be defrayed out of "a gift of certain lands to the value yearly of xlvi*li*. iij*s*. ij*d*. ob. [£46 : 3 : 2½]," made by the king to the burgesses. This "school at Stratord," we learn from Strype, "was the last this prince founded." The endowment is not yet exhausted, although the corporation, after the duke's execution, took to itself the government of the school; and the boys of Stratford still enjoy the advantages of Edward VI's foundation. The schoolhouse stood as it stands to-day with slight alteration, under the shadow of the guild chapel, forming part of the buildings of the old guild in Church Street. The schoolrooms were reached from an inner yard by an external staircase "roofed with tile," which was demolished about fifty years ago. Above them was a "soller" —a still higher story or garret—which was taken down in 1568. The fabric of the house, which had seen service in the days of the ancient guild, was old and in need of repair in Shakespeare's boyhood; and in 1568 it underwent several amendments. A few years later the rooms became uninhabitable and underwent further renovation. While they were under repair the master had to take his pupils into the chapel itself. This was probably not an uncommon practice. Shakespeare likened Malvolio to "a pedant that keeps school i' the church." But in 1595 the holding of school in church or chapel was forbidden for the future.

To this school the children of the Stratford freemen were sent, with rare exceptions. It was one of those "common schools" that received, according to a contemporary account, "all sorts of children to be taught, be their parents never so poor and the boys never so unapt." And from Henley Street, some three hundred yards away, came each morning, from

1571 onwards, William, the seven-year-old son of John Shakespeare. His description penned thirty years later of

> The whining schoolboy, with his satchel,
> And shining morning face, creeping like snail
> Unwillingly to school,

is doubtless a reminiscence of this daily walk.

The education supplied at a free day-school in Elizabethan England depended largely on the attainments of the schoolmaster, and these varied very much in quality with times and places. According to many contemporary writers, bad schoolmasters prevailed. " It is a general plague and complaint of the whole land," writes Peacham in the seventeenth century, "for, for one discreet and able teacher, you shall find twenty ignorant and careless; who (among so many fertile and delicate wits as *England* affordeth), whereas they make one scholar, they mar ten;" and Roger Ascham had written some years before in the same strain. In many towns the office of schoolmaster was conferred on "an ancient citizen of no great learning." Sometimes a quack conjuring doctor, like Pinch, of the *Comedy of Errors*, held the post. An eccentric master of St. Alban's School in

Domestic and School Discipline 175

the middle of the sixteenth century paid so much deference to the parents of his pupils, that "by no entreaty would [he] teach any scholar he had further than his father had learned before them." He argued that they would then prove saucy rogues and control their fathers. From the comparatively small number of burgesses at Stratford who could sign their names in the middle of the sixteenth century, we may infer that William Dalam, the last master appointed by the ancient guild, was no very zealous or capable performer of the duties of the office. But the far smaller average of marksmen in subsequent years proves that Dalam's successors were fairly discreet and able pedagogues. The burgesses seem to have carefully selected them, and to have taken them on trial for two years at a time, and Walter Roche, appointed in 1570, Thomas Hunt in 1577, and Thomas Jenkins in 1580, apparently satisfied all the burgesses' requirements.

The scholiasts have waxed warm in controversy over the educational equipment bestowed on the poet at Stratford; and while one has denied him the veriest elementary knowledge of the classics, another has credited him with the acquirements of a Bentley or a Porson. There is every reason to believe that Masters Roche and Hunt gave young Shakespeare and his schoolfellows a firm grasp of Latin at least, and led them from the accidence and Lilly's grammar through conversation books and colloquies, like the *Sententiæ Pueriles*, up to Horace, Seneca, and Plautus, and "the rest of the finest Latin poets," of whom conscientious masters were advised by contemporary writers on education to give their pupils a taste. It is just possible that at the most efficient country schools the more advanced scholars, before the patronage of some neighbouring magnate or the bestowal of a college scholarship enabled them to proceed to the universities, learnt something of the Greek grammar, with the Greek Testament, and Isocrates or Demosthenes. But Shakespeare was doubtless withdrawn from school, in consequence of his father's pecuniary misfortunes, before he enjoyed these advantages.

In the pedantic Holofernes of *Love's Labour's Lost*, Shakespeare has carefully portrayed the best type of the rural schoolmaster, as in Pinch he has portrayed the worst, and the freshness and fulness of detail imparted to the former portrait may easily lead to the conclusion that its author was drawing upon his own experience. Holofernes does not long appear on the stage before he pompously quotes from Lilly's grammar: "Vir sapit qui pauca loquitur." Other of Holofernes's phrases illustrate the practice in vogue of inviting boys to supply English synonyms to Latin words proposed by the master. His words, "*sanguis*, blood, . . . *cœlum*, the sky, the welkin, the heaven, . . . *terra*, the soil, the land, the earth," are veritable extracts from phrase-books like the *Sententiæ Pueriles*, which lads had to learn by heart. The formal dialogue in which Holofernes and his friend the curate, Sir Nathaniel, engage—

> *Hol.* Novi hominem tanquam te : anne intelligis?
> *Nath.* Laus Deo, bene intelligo.
> *Nath.* Videsne quis venit?
> *Hol.* Video et gaudeo.

is framed on models, to be met with in many popular Elizabethan school-books of familiar dialogues. And Shakespeare elsewhere proves his intimacy with the dialogue in such volumes specially marked for use in a school, when he makes Holofernes allude to their common phrases—

He speaks false Latin. *Diminuit Prisciani caput.*
It is barbarous Latin. *Olet barbariem*—

in the criticism of Sir Nathaniel's Latin as "Priscian a little scratched," and in the remark, "I smell false Latin," on the country clown's burlesque misreading of "ad dunghill" for "ad unguem." The pedagogue's citation of a line and a half from "the good old Mantuan" (the mediæval poet Mantuanus, whose eclogues, often preferred to Virgil's in the sixteenth century, formed the chief study of the fourth form in many grammar schools), his attempts to recall his Horace, his praises of Ovid as the writer whose works were to be studied by Latin verse-makers, may all fairly be interpreted as memories of the instruction given at Stratford.

It was usual for a boy to remain at the grammar school for seven years at least, from the age of seven to that of fourteen, and unless the master was singularly incapable, and the boys singularly rebellious, it was seldom that a young Elizabethan failed to acquire some useful knowledge in his schooldays. He rarely left school without being able to "write and read English and congrue Latin." But schoolboy morality was not very high, and by the practice of little

THE GRAMMAR SCHOOL.

frauds it was possible, we learn from contemporary sources, for idle pupils to make "shift to escape correction" without making any progress at the schoolhouse. An ingenious device of "prompting" one another was practised by boys, born in the same year as young Shakespeare, at Gloucester Grammar School; a few pupils would prepare the lesson given them overnight, and "being at the elbows" of their idle companions, would put into their mouths answers to their master's question as he walked up and down by them. One of the boys named Willis has amusingly recounted his own experience of this system. After pursuing it for a long while with complete success, "it fell out on a day that one of the eldest scholars and one of the highest form fell out with me upon occasion of some boys' play abroad," and all help from the prompters was denied him. His companions looked forward to seeing him "fall under the rod," but he gathered all his wits together, began to study for himself, and "so the evil intended to me by my fellow-scholar, turned to my great good." Small frauds of this kind were encouraged by the severity of the discipline adopted in all the rural schools. The birch was in continual request, and was administered with alarming brutality. Roger Ascham has described how recklessly floggings were awarded at Eton, and in the smaller schools the masters were under less intelligent supervision. A repulsive picture of the terrors which the schoolhouse had for a nervous child is drawn in a "pretie and merry new interlude," entitled "The Disobedient Child, compiled by Thomas Ingelend, late student in Cambridge," about 1560. A boy who implores his father not to force him to go to school, tells of his companions' sufferings there—how

> Their tender bodies both night and day
> Are whipped and scourged, and beat like a stone,
> That from top to toe the skin is away;

and a story is repeated of how a scholar was tormented to death by "his bloody master." Other accounts show that the playwright has not gone far beyond the fact. Peacham describes a schoolmaster with whom he was acquainted, "who in winter would ordinarily, on a cold morning, whip his boys even for no other purpose than to get himself a heat." Nevertheless, we believe that Masters Roche and Hunt were of a milder disposition. Holofernes, although of a dry humour, seems well disposed towards his pupils, and is invited in the play to dine with the father of one of them. Sir Hugh Evans asks his pupil, William Page, "some questions in his accidence," when he meets him and his mother on a school holiday, with a geniality that makes it probable that his creator knew many of his profession who wielded the rod with discrimination.

XVII

THE OCCUPATIONS OF STRATFORD LADS

A FEW lads on leaving school passed on to the universities, or inns of court, to proceed in the study of the common law, divinity, or physic. Rich parents were usually anxious to give their children an opportunity of pursuing an academic career. At both Oxford and Cambridge charitable endowments maintained at the same time a large number of poor scholars. Sir Hugh Clopton had, as we have seen, left money for such a purpose. Of the poor university scholars, the majority entered the Church, and a great number of them gained high preferment there. Their wealthier companions usually sought their fortunes at the bar, or after living riotously in London, often swelled the band of military adventurers by sea and land.

But the larger proportion of the boys of a rural grammar school looked forward to earning a livelihood by trade in their native town. And it was not an infrequent objection urged by practical men against the seven or eight years spent by the lads at school, that the time might have been better occupied in teaching them "a mystery or occupation." When a boy's schooldays were over, it was usual for his father to apprentice him to himself if an eldest son, or to a neighbour if a younger one, and seven years were consumed in the process of learning a trade. The restrictions on trading at the time rendered this step incumbent on any parent who valued his son's future prosperity. No man who had not undergone a legally recognised apprenticeship was permitted by the municipal laws to open a shop or practise any craft within the borough, or to exercise any of the rights of a freeman. "No person," ran an order issued by the burgesses of Stratford on 13th April 1603, "shall set up, occupy, or exercise any trade, mystery, or occupation before he be made free or confirmed in his freedom of the same trade whereunto he was apprentice." In all towns the apprentices formed the least orderly portion of the population, and the regulations enforced against them at Stratford—that they were to be at home before nine o'clock at night, that they were never to wear swords, and that they were not to tipple at the alehouses— prove that the older burgesses had some experience of their irregularities. Many of them spent three days and three nights in the stocks for breaches of the municipal bye-laws.

Whether or no Shakespeare on quitting school became an ordinary apprentice ("he was formerly in this town," wrote Aubrey, "bound apprentice to a butcher," *i.e.* apprentice to his father), there can be little doubt that the apprentices whom he had known at school were his intimate companions in early manhood. The tradition recorded by Aubrey distinctly states that "there was at that time another butcher's son in this town, that was held not at all inferior to him for a natural wit, his acquaintance and coetanean, but died young."

In September 1585, when the Earl of Leicester sent letters to his friends round Kenilworth to enlist 500 men for the army which he was leading to the Low Countries, some adventurous ne'er-do-weels of Stratford doubtless shouldered a pike beneath their great neighbour's standard. Stratford names like Combe and Arden certainly figure in the muster-lists of Leicester's battalions.

Shakespeare's intimate knowledge of the technicalities of warfare has led one writer to the inference that Shakespeare himself marched with his young townsmen under Leicester's banner. A vain attempt has indeed been made to identify him with "Will, my Lord of Leicester's jesting player," who (we know on the authority of Sir Philip Sidney) accompanied Leicester to Holland.

Some of Shakespeare's schoolfellows found more peaceful occupation in the great houses of the country gentlemen in the neighbourhood of Stratford. It was their custom to keep a large retinue of serving-men—"comely men, and commonly sons of honest yeomen or farmers of the country"—who led a lazy life in the manor-houses, wearing good garments or liveries, aiding in their master's sports, and attending him at his meals. They were skilled, as a rule, in wrestling, leaping, running, and dancing; they could shoot with the long-bow or cross-bow, handle guns well, and entertain their masters with table-talk about hawks, hounds, fishing, and agriculture. Their profession brought them in some forty pounds a year, besides a good livery with a badge upon it, and in their master's absence they were wont to entertain their own guests in his hall. The menial servants—the bakers, brewers, chamberlains, wardrobers, falconers, hunters, horse-keepers, lackeys, fools, cooks, scullions, hog-herds, and the like—were far below them in social status. Shakespeare introduces serving-men on the stage as the confidants of their masters in the persons of Tranio and Balthasar; and Malvolio, Olivia's steward, was of their class. The author of an interesting tract, entitled "The English Courtier and Country Gentleman" (1586), which deals largely with "the superfluity of serving-men" kept in country houses, designates them as so much unprofitable furniture, and points out how they were proud and ill-natured, and wasted their master's substance.

Of the houses near Stratford into which young townsmen were received, the nearest was doubtless Clopton House. At Charlecote Sir Thomas

Lucy, at Milcote Sir Edward Greville, and at Long Compton Lord Compton maintained large establishments; while at no great distance was the castle of Kenilworth, in the occupation for the greater part of Elizabeth's reign of the Earl of Leicester. At these great buildings Shakespeare in all probability frequently visited schoolfellows who had secured places in their owners' retinues.

But there were young Stratford men who had higher aspirations than life in the town itself or in the immediate neighbourhood could satisfy. Life in London, then as now, was the goal of much youthful ambition, and thither occasionally youths from Stratford made their way to seek fame or fortune, or both. John Sadler was one of these in Shakespeare's time, and an account of his early life is interesting. On quitting Stratford he "joined himself to the carrier, and came to London, where he had never been before, and sold his horse in Smithfield; and having no acquaintance in London to recommend him or assist him, he went from street to street, and house to house, asking if they wanted an apprentice, and though he met with many discouraging scorns and a thousand denials, he went on till he lighted on Mr. Brokesbank, a grocer in Bucklersbury, who, though he long denied him for want of sureties for his fidelity, and because the money he had (but ten pounds) was so disproportionable to what he used to receive with apprentices, yet, upon his discreet account he gave of himself and the motives which put him upon that course, and promise to compensate with diligent and faithful service whatever else was short of his expectation, he ventured to receive him upon trial, in which he so well approved himself that he accepted him into his service, to which he bound him for eight years."

Another native of Stratford who sought an apprenticeship in London was Richard Field, son of that Henry Field, tanner, of whose property an inventory was made by his friend, John Shakespeare, in 1592. Richard Field was apprenticed to a printer in London in 1579, and in 1587 set up in business for himself. It is of interest to note that in 1593 he printed his fellow-townsman's "Venus and Adonis," and later his "Rape of Lucrece."

There is a current tradition that certain actors who acquired Elizabethan fame were natives of Stratford, and sought admission to a company of players on its visit to the town during a provincial tour. Thomas Greene and the two Burbages, James and Richard, have been claimed by the borough's historians as Shakespeare's fellow-townsmen; but in no case has the evidence proved conclusive. Nevertheless, it is certain that Stratford was visited with sufficient frequency by the London actors to induce some young men there, who were weary of their long apprenticeships to look in the direction of the drama for relief from uncongenial occupations. Of these young men William Shakespeare was probably one. Of his mode of life between 1578 and 1585, it may be stated as fairly certain that his father, during that period, endeavoured to secure his services in rehabilitating his decaying trade; that William took unkindly to the pursuit of woolstapling in all its manifold branches; that he believed himself capable of making his way as actor and playwright; and that he set out for London to try his fortune in these professions.

XVIII

THE PLAYERS AT STRATFORD

IF John Shakespeare ever regretted—as many a sober citizen of the day might have done—his son's choice of this primrose path, he had only himself to blame. Like all his friends of the town council, he was undoubtedly a lover of plays. While he was bailiff in 1568-69, he granted licenses to play in the town to the Queen's players and the Earl of Worcester's players, two of the chief companies. Nine times between 1573 and 1581 did these or other companies enter the town with drum and trumpet, wearing their noble masters' badge, and give their performances in the guildhall. Very few of the town chamberlains down to the close of the century failed to enter in their annual accounts an item varying very capriciously from nine pounds to twelvepence paid for dramatic entertainments at the fair time in September. In 1597 payments were made to four companies. Every manner of show could, in fact, reckon on a good reception in Stratford; and in 1597 the bailiff sent three shillings and fourpence to a man bringing to the town his puppet show of the city of Norwich, a famous show to which the dramatists often made allusion.

Shakespeare as a child undoubtedly witnessed such performances; and the circumstantial account given by a Gloucester contemporary named Willis—born in the same year as the poet—of his father's practice of taking him to the play, may well apply to William Shakespeare. The plays Willis witnessed were interludes—brief moralities with the faintest semblance of a plot about them. When the players came to a town, he tells us, they first waited on the mayor or bailiff to inform him "what nobleman's servants they were, and so get license for their public playing." If the mayor liked the players, or wished to show their master respect, he would invite them to play for their first performance in the guildhall before himself and the aldermen. "That is called the mayor's play, when every one that will comes in without money, the mayor giving the players as he thinks to show respect unto them." Afterwards they would perform in the courtyard of an inn, as at the Swan, Bear, or Crown, in Bridge Street, Stratford, and charge for admission. Willis, according to his own account, witnessed the mayor's play, standing between his father's legs, "while he sat upon one of the benches, and where we saw and heard very well." The interlude performed was the "Cradle of Security," in which the chief characters were the Wicked of the World, Pride, Covetousness, Luxury, the End of the World, and the Last Judgment. "The sight," Willis adds, "took such impression on me that when I came to man's estate, it was as fresh in my memory as if I had seen it newly acted." It is quite possible, moreover, that John Shakespeare occasionally took his son over to Coventry to witness the famous miracles or mysteries on Corpus Christi Day — the Thursday after Trinity Sunday.

The Stratford townsfolk had from an early period been wont to witness these performances. In *The Hundred Merry Tales*, first issued in 1526, a popular jest-book of the sixteenth century, whence Beatrice taunts Benedick with having borrowed his wit, there is the story of a Warwickshire village priest, who concluded a sermon on the twelve articles of the creed with the words, "If you believe not me, then for a more surety and sufficient authority, go your way to Coventry, and there ye shall see them all played in Corpus Christi play." There Shakespeare, in all probability, learned how a grotesquely-painted canvas face, through whose open mouth a fire was visible, satisfactorily represented Hell in the popular view. There he doubtless made the acquaintance of the sooty-faced figures that stood for lost souls, of Herod in his many-coloured dress and flaming sword, and of the Devil and his tormentor the Vice. That the poet knew these features of the mysteries and something of their machinery, is clear from such references as Falstaff's comparison of the flea on Bardolph's nose to "a black soul burning in hell," or Hamlet's advice to the players to avoid inexplicable dumb-shows and noise that out-herods Herod, or the Clown's description in *Twelfth Night* of the "old Vice,"

> Who, with dagger of lath,
> In his rage and his wrath,
> Cries, ah, ha! to the devil.

It may be that among the Stratford people themselves, as in other towns and villages, pageants of rudimentary dramatic interest were played by the "bachelry" at Christmas or Whitsuntide. In *Love's Labour's Lost* the show of the "Nine Worthies," presented by the schoolmaster and his companions, has all the features of a rural Christmas comedy, and the "Pyramus and Thisbe" of *Midsummer Night's Dream* is constructed and presented by "hard-handed men,"

> Which never laboured in their minds till now,
> And now have toiled their unbreathed memories
> With this same play.

A similar entertainment is described by Julia in the *Two Gentlemen of Verona*, another of Shakespeare's earliest comedies, when she, disguised as a page, is enlisting Silvia's sympathy in her own behalf. "At Pentecost," she says,

> When all our pageants of delight were play'd,
> Our youth got me to play the woman's part,

The Players at Stratford

And I was trimm'd in madam Julia's gown;
Which served me as fit, by all men's judgments,
As if the garment had been made for me: . . .
    For I did play a lamentable part:
    Madam, 'twas Ariadne, passioning
For Theseus' perjury, and unjust flight.

Pageants and interludes were played at intervals at the neighbouring great country houses, where, as in the *Taming of the Shrew* and *Hamlet*, strolling companies often offered their services; and there is reason to believe that Shakespeare's father took him when eleven years old to Kenilworth, to witness the elaborate performances arranged to honour the Queens' visit there to Lord Leicester in 1575. Every step that Elizabeth took on this occasion was celebrated by some quaint semi-dramatic device. As she first approached the castle on Saturday, the 9th of July, a Sibyl met her, prophesying prosperity to her government. The porter who opened the gate to her was disguised as Hercules. When she passed a pond in the outer court, female figures personating water nymphs offered her welcome. Next day a display of fireworks took place. Monday was occupied in hunting, ingeniously diversified by a sylvan masque. In whatever direction the Queen rode in the neighbouring country during the ensuing week, the villagers arranged similar shows for her delight. Reminiscences of these pageants have been detected by the commentators on *Midsummer Night's Dream*, in Oberon's famous description, of the whereabouts of the little western flower, Love-in-idleness.

XIX

RURAL SPORTS

THUS we may receive without much misgiving the theory that Shakespeare was encouraged while still a boy at Stratford to honour the drama; and that it was in accordance with an early ambition that he sought employment in 1585 at a London playhouse. But the drama was not the only amusement in which Shakespeare's plays prove him to have taken part; there are many indications that, as a youth, he practised all manner of rural sports, and did not always escape censure in pursuit of them. Many of them he doubtless engaged in far from Stratford, for he had many relatives among the farmers of the district, and they all encouraged young men in athletic exercises. His grandmother, Agnes Arden, was still living at Wilmecote, and his father's brother, Henry, was still farming at Snitterfield.

Rustic games for all ages and dispositions are mentioned in Shakespeare's plays. In his early comedies he refers to the "whipping of tops," "hide and seek," "more sacks to the mill," "pushpin," and "nine men's morris." The last, a game played on turf, seems to have resembled "fox and geese," now played with marbles on a wooden board. "Nine-pins" or "ten-pins," "quoits," "hockey," "football," "leap-frog," "country base" or "prisoner's base," "fast and loose," and "flap-dragon," are also among the rural diversions of Elizabethan days to which Shakespeare makes allusion. Bowls formed a more solemn urban recreation, and the town council maintained a bowling alley for the free use of the townsmen, while they provided at the public expense at least one top for the boys. At Whitsuntide, or the beginning of May, there were village dances about the may-pole in which young and old took part, "busied with a Whitsun morris-dance."

Even John Shakespeare, like the franklin described by Sir Thomas Overbury, doubtless "allowed of honest pastime, and thought not the bones of the dead anything bruised, or the worse for it, though the country lasses danced in the churchyard after evensong." Probably, also, " Rock-Monday, and the wake in summer, Shrovings, the wakeful catches on Christmas eve, the hoky or seed-cake, these he yearly kept, yet held them no relics of Popery." Rock-Monday followed Twelfth Day, and celebrated the resumption of the distaff or rock by the housewives after the twelve days' festivities at Christmas time. Shrove Tuesday, when apprentices made holiday, was chiefly consecrated to pancakes, cockfights, and cockthrowing. Hock-tide, the Monday and Tuesday after the second Sunday following Easter, was devoted to banquetings and to sports, like wrestling, hurling, and shooting at the butts. At Coventry the Corpus Christi play was often repeated then, or one of rougher merriment performed. Harvest homes were also honoured with like celebration, and especially with "barley-break," a game played by lads and lasses in the cornfields, which seems to have roughly resembled prisoner's base. Then it was that

> Corin sat all day
> Playing on pipes of corn, and versing love
> To amorous Phillida.

Bearbaitings occasionally diversified the amusements of the country side, and in morris-dancing the young people often indulged on "the wanton green" of a summer's evening.

From an early date far-famed athletic meetings took place on the Cotswold Hills, at which Will Squeele, according to Justice Shallow, was a "swinge-buckler." The Cotswold games were greatly improved by one Captain Dover, of Barton-on-the-Heath, not far from Stratford, early in James I.'s reign; and coursing with greyhounds was pursued there. Shakespeare clearly knew these coursing matches well. He makes Slender ask John Page, "How does your fallow greyhound? I heard say, he was outrun at Cotsale."

Of more elaborate country sports with which Shakespeare was clearly well acquainted, although he probably in early life witnessed them from afar, hunting and hawking hold the chief place. "An' a man have not skill in the hawking and hunting languages, I'll not give a rush for him," says Master Stephen in Jonson's

Every Man in his Humour; and there is no lack of evidence that Shakespeare studied them both. He clearly had an ear for the music of the hounds, and often marked

> The musical confusion
> Of hounds and echo in conjunction.

Theseus knows what hounds should be :—

> My hounds (he says) are bred out of the Spartan kind,
> So flew'd, so sanded : and their heads are hung
> With ears that sweep away the morning dew ;
> Crook-kneed, and dew-lapp'd like Thessalian bulls,
> Slow in pursuit, but match'd in mouth like bells,
> Each under each. A cry more tunable
> Was never holla'd to, nor cheer'd with horn.

Near Stratford too, Shakespeare doubtless learnt the famous song of the hunt, to which he alludes in *Romeo and Juliet* :—

> The hunt is up, the hunt is up,
> Sing merrily we, the hunt is up :
> The birds they sing,
> The deer they fling,
> Hey ninny, ninny no.

" The noble art of venery " was often pursued in enclosed parks by the owners of the great houses, with trains of ladies, foresters, and other retainers. Deer was their chief quarry, and cross-bows seem to have then vied with hounds in bringing down the prey. It is this method of hunting that Shakespeare elaborately describes in *Love's Labour's Lost*, when the Princess and her ladies hunt the deer in the King of Navarre's park. But the stag chase and the boar chase were pursued in the open country. It is over "a poor sequester'd stag that from the hunter's aim had ta'en a hurt," that Jaques moralises in well-known lines. In his "Venus and Adonis" Shakespeare especially recommends the hunting of the hare, the fox, and the roe; and in another famous passage of this first poem he describes all the points of a hunter. It is very possible that Shakespeare in youth chased the timorous hare on foot. No more vivid picture of the pursuit of "poor Wat" is found in literature than in Shakespeare's "Venus and Adonis." He shows us there the poor wretch "outrunning the wind," "cranking and crossing with a thousand doubles," eluding the cunning hounds among a flock of sheep or herd of deer, or "where earth-delving conies keep," then far off upon a hill "standing on hinder legs with listening ear"—

> To hearken if his foes pursue him still;
> Anon their loud alarums he doth hear;

MARY ARDEN'S COTTAGE AT WILMECOTE.

> And now his grief may be compared well
> To one sore sick, that hears the passing bell.

Hawking—"a princely delight," as one contemporary writer calls it, or "a pleasure for high and mounting spirits," according to another authority — was a more elaborate sport than hunting, and was invariably confined to the rich, although the country people delighted to watch its practice of a winter's morning, or to listen by night to the falconers' stories of their hawks' prowess. Similes and metaphors without number has Shakespeare drawn from this recreation, and his continual use of its technical terms, all of which are now obsolete, accounts for the obscurity of many passages in his plays. Hawks went by a variety of names, according to their age and training, and Shakespeare uses them all. There was the wild and incorrigible haggard, to which Petruchio likens his shrew, Katharine:—

> Another way I have to man my haggard,
> To make her come, and know her keeper's call;
> That is,—to watch her as we watch these kites,
> That bate, and beat, and will not be obedient.

(To bate is to flutter the wings.) There was the eyas-musket, *i.e.* the hawk in its infancy, and the tassel-gentle, the mate of the goss-hawk, to both of which frequent allusion is made by the dramatist. Shakespeare knew how the hawks were unhooded and whistled off the fist, to which jesses and lures attached them, or how, when they were incapable of benefiting at the trainer's hands, they were let down the wind. Probably, too, Shakespeare was not unacquainted with less dignified sport in which birds were the prey. He talks of "bat-fowling," which is a Cotswold expression for taking birds by night in hand-nets, and of "setting springes for woodcocks." "The creeping fowler," at a time when shooting birds was not a legitimate pastime, often succeeded, according to a passage in *Midsummer Night's Dream*, in doing something more than scatter by his gun's report wild geese or russet-pated choughs.

The Avon, with its "wind'ring brooks, with their sedg'd crowns and ever harmless nooks," must have also introduced the Elizabethan dwellers to some river sport. The river was not made navigable for even small boats till 1635, and rowing as a recreation grew up at a much later date. But fishing has always had its

English votaries. Few of the mediæval monasteries in this country lacked their anglers; and the literature of the sixteenth century was graced by many tributes of no mean value to "an exercise so much laudable." The incidental references that Shakespeare makes to the angler's art, the poetic fulness of his descriptions of the banks and "fair course" of rivers, and the distinctness with which he occasionally speaks of various freshwater fish, makes it almost certain that he himself, like others of his townsmen, had trolled for pike or luces, and tickled trout—for in those days fly-fishing was not—in the Warwickshire or Gloucestershire streams. If the Avon then, as now, only harboured fish of the rank of dace and bream, pike and perch, the Elizabethan angler had but to make his way from Stratford to the streams that run from the Cotswolds into the Severn or the sources of the Thames, to enter a paradise where trout seldom failed him. Within a few miles of Stratford lived one of the most enthusiastic anglers of Shakespeare's time—a Gloucestershire squire named John Dennis, who gave voice to his passion in a long poem called the "Secrets of Angling," first published in

P

1613. In these verses the joys of the angler are extolled above those of any other sportsman, and the author details the pleasures that he had experienced of seeing his " quill and cork down sink, with eager bite of barbel, bleak, or dace." If Shakespeare, who described how

> The pleasant'st angling is to see the fish
> Cut with her golden oars the silver stream,
> And greedily devour the treacherous bait,

ever lived in his youth at Dursley, as many writers have urged, he surely helped Dennis to fish his waters, whether with or without his permission.

XX

CHARLECOTE HOUSE—POACHING IN THE PARK

IF tradition be admitted in evidence, the poet did not on occasion disdain to play the poacher. According to the ancient story, the whole course of his life was altered by his detection in the act of poaching at Charlecote Park. "The frolic of Shakespeare in deer-stealing was the cause of his Hegira," says Landor, and although there is something to be urged against this statement, it probably has some foundation in fact.

Tourists seldom leave Shakespeare's native place without traversing the four or five miles to the north-east which lie between it and the great park encircling Charlecote House.[1] The winding River Avon skirts the enclosure to the

---

[1] This chapter is chiefly from two papers which I contributed to the *Portfolio* for May and July 1888.

west. Large herds of deer are now always crouching under the branches of the old oaks and elms within its timber boundaries. The gray-red mansion where the Lucys have lived for more than three centuries stands at the water's edge; avenues of limes approach it at back and front; the flower-gardens which immediately surround it are separated from the gently undulating park by a sunken fence. The present century has witnessed many additions to the building, but the Elizabethan portion has not been disfigured by restoration, and from one aspect still seems to the visitor to stand detached from the recent erections. Nowhere is a more finished specimen of Tudor domestic architecture to be met with.

The building of the Elizabethan house at Charlecote was begun in 1558 — the year of Elizabeth's accession — and was probably finished in 1559. Its owner was Thomas Lucy. For more than five centuries his ancestors had owned the Charlecote Manor, which had figured in Domesday Book under the name of Ceorlecote. At first the lords of the manor took their surname from the place, but early in the thirteenth century William de Charlecote, who had fought with the Barons against King John, assumed, for reasons which antiquaries have not determined, the name of Lucy. A manor-house, with a chapel attached, was in existence at Charlecote throughout the Middle Ages, and its owners' prosperity grew, chiefly through intermarriages, with every generation. One Fulk de Lucy, who died in 1303, was "a special lover of good horses," and paid forty marks (*i.e.* £26 : 13 : 4) for a black horse at a time when an ox cost sixteen shillings. Many of his descendants sat in Parliament as knights of the shire of Warwick, and nearly all of them, for military services rendered to the Crown at home or abroad, received the honour of knighthood. William Lucy became a Knight of the Bath when Henry VII's Queen Elizabeth was crowned at Westminster, and it was Sir William's grandson who built Charlecote as we know it.

The young man had been carefully brought up. John Foxe, the compiler of the martyrology, had come from Oxford to be his tutor, and on 3d February 1547 (it is of interest to note) Foxe, while holding that office, married at the little Charlecote church Agnes Randall, a lady of many virtues, who was, like himself, in the service of the Lucy's.[1] Foxe's pupil was only twenty-six years old when he took the work of rebuilding Charlecote in hand, but six years earlier, in 1552, his father's death had made him master of his family's great Warwickshire estate, which soon included, besides Charlecote, the neighbouring properties of Sherborne and Hampton Lucy, the former a grant of Edward VI, and the latter of Queen Mary in 1556. Meanwhile his wife, Joyce Acton, had brought him Sutton Park, at Tenbury, Worcestershire. His worldly position was in no wise inferior to that of a nobleman; and he was wealthy enough to freely indulge the taste for elaborate architecture which characterised the aristocracy of his day.

Of the pre-Elizabethan manor-house at Charlecote no trace remains. The Elizabethan mansion, reared probably on the old site, owes nothing to an earlier epoch. The ground-plan roughly resembles the letter E, an eccentric compliment which great builders of the day were fond of paying to the reigning sovereign. The original building, with its gently sloping

[1] See Art. "Foxe, John," in *Dictionary of National Biography*.

gables, is flanked at either end by boldly projecting wings, with octagonal angle turrets. The fabric is of red brick; the window dressings are of stone, but all has grown greyish with age. Near the centre of the façade stands an elaborate porch, which supplies on the ground-plan the E's short middle stroke. There is a striking contrast between this richly worked excrescence and the homely simplicity of the rest of the building. It has been suggested that it was by a different and more fashionable architect, who was acquainted with both the Italian and French Renaissance styles, and that it was added after the house was built. John of Padua, *alias* John Thorpe, the designer of Holland House and the greatest English architect of the time, is credited on uncertain grounds with this admirable specimen of Renaissance architecture. It is in two floors, each supported by pillars, and the whole surmounted by a delicately carved balustrade. The front is of freestone; the lower pillars are of the Ionic order, the upper of the Composite. Over the doorway, on the ground story, the royal arms, with the letters 'E.R.' are engraved,

and in the spandrils are the initial letters
'T.L.,' *i.e.* Thomas Lucy.

But the porch is not the only remarkable feature of the exterior of Charlecote. Before the house lies a quadrangular garden court enclosed by low terrace walls, protected from without by the sunken fence. On the side of the enclosure that is farthest from the house rises a massive structure two storeys high, and completely isolated. Through its ground-floor runs a narrow archway, closed at the outward end by iron gates. This structure is the detached gatehouse, of which few examples remain in England. In earlier Tudor times large mansions were usually quadrangular in shape, like the colleges at Oxford and Cambridge. In that case the gatehouse invariably surmounted the one archway by which the quadrangle could be entered. It was at times battlemented and fortified to resist attack, but more often architects lavished on it their most elaborate schemes of decoration. When the quadrangular form of building was dying out its memory occasionally survived in a forecourt fronted by an isolated building, exactly modelled after the older fashioned

CHARLECOTE PARK.

gatehouse; but now that three sides of the quadrangle were absent, it stood, as here at Charlecote, at some fifty yards' distance from the mansion, looking like a stately lodge.

In its architecture the gatehouse at Charlecote exactly resembles the main building. Octagonal turrets adorn its four angles. Its roof is flat, and is surmounted by a balustrade; oriel windows project on the second floor above both ends of the archway. In Elizabethan days the porter lived on the ground floor; the upper formed a large banqueting-room. As a defence against unwelcome intruders the gatehouse still had its uses, but great householders had long ceased to fear very formidable foes in Elizabeth's time; and it was probably erected by Sir Thomas Lucy merely as an effective architectural ornament.

Comparatively little within the house to-day recalls the sixteenth century. But in the library stand chairs, couch, and cabinet of coromandel wood, inlaid with ivory, which, tradition says, were presented by Queen Elizabeth to Leicester in 1575, and were brought here from Kenilworth in the seventeenth century.[1]

The modern bust of the poet in the hall recalls the relationship which tradition has set up between Sir Thomas Lucy, its builder, and the dramatist in his youth. By 1586 or 1587, when the two men are alleged to have become acquainted, Thomas Lucy had grown in dignity. Six years after he had completed the rebuilding of his manor-house, he was knighted (in 1565), and he subsequently sat in two parliaments (1571 and 1584) as knight of the shire of Warwick. In 1586 he was high sheriff of the neighbouring county of Worcestershire, in right of the property derived from his wife. The town of Stratford-on-Avon knew him well. As a local justice and commissioner of the musters for the county of Warwick, he frequently rode thither, and the Corporation liberally entertained him at the Bear or the Swan, the chief inns of the city. But these performances never made a man famous. Had not tradition credited Sir Thomas Lucy with preserving deer in Charle-

---

[1] An interesting account of Charlecote appears in Mr. W. Niven's privately printed *Old Warwickshire House* (1878).

cote Park, and accused the poet Shakespeare of poaching on his preserves, there would have been no reason why his name should have escaped obscurity. It is stated that he entertained Queen Elizabeth on her way to the great entertainment provided for her at Kenilworth by Leicester in 1575. But it is impossible that the Queen could have slept there, for her authentic route is known, and does not include Charlecote as a resting-place at night. Some urge modestly that she breakfasted there, but this report lacks confirmation.

In the seventeenth century it was currently reported in Stratford that Shakespeare as a youth fell into bad company, and "made a frequent practice of deer-stealing . . . more than once . . . robbing a park that belonged to Sir Thomas Lucy of Charlecote, near Stratford." On one occasion, according to the version recorded by Rowe, the earliest editor of the plays, he was arrested by Sir Thomas's keeper and severely punished, whereupon "he made a ballad upon" the owner of Charlecote, which was "probably the first essay of his poetry." Further persecution was threatened, and Shakespeare escaped to London to try his fortune on the stage. The independent testimony of Archdeacon Davies, who was vicar of Saperton, Gloucestershire, late in the seventeenth century, is to the effect that Shakespeare "was much given to all unluckiness in stealing venison and rabbits, particularly from Sir Thomas Lucy, who had him oft whipped, and sometimes imprisoned, and at last made him fly his native county to his great advancement." The soundest scholar among Shakespeare's biographers—Mr. Halliwell-Phillipps—accepts the outline of this story as incontrovertible fact. The additional details that Queen Elizabeth intervened to protect Shakespeare from Sir Thomas's fury, and that the youth stole the buck to celebrate his wedding-day, are obvious fabrications. Nor can the rumour—perpetuated in a well-known picture—that Shakespeare when arrested by the keepers was brought before Sir Thomas in the hall of Charlecote be substantiated.

It has been urged by disbelievers in the whole tradition that in the sixteenth century no deer-park existed at Charlecote. There was, however, a recognised warren at Charle-

THE GRAND HALL AT CHARLECOTE.

cote, and in the view of the law the theft of rabbits from a statutable warren was as serious an offence as deer-stealing, and might easily have been confused with it. According to Coke, a warren might be inhabited by hares and roes as well as by rabbits, and Shakespeare might thus have sought his prey in Lucy's warren without seriously impugning the truth of the tradition. But although Charlecote in Shakespeare's youth cannot be proved to have been a statutable park—*i.e.* an enclosure "closed with wall, pale, or hedge," and "used for the keeping, breeding, and cherishing of deer"—Sir Thomas is known to have been an extensive game-preserver, and to have employed gamekeepers on many of his estates. In March 1585 he introduced a Bill into Parliament for the better preservation of "game and grain." He did not, it is true, make many recorded gifts of venison; but a German traveller in Elizabeth's reign noted that fallow-deer of various colours were as commonly met with in England in woods as in enclosed parks, and there seems no doubt that deer lived in Hampton Woods in the immediate neighbourhood of Charlecote. When, in the seventeenth century, Sir Thomas's successor acquired Fulbroke Park, which also lies on the boundaries of Charlecote, he is stated on good authority to have immediately stocked it with deer. And as early as 1602 the Lord Keeper, Egerton, received a buck from the Lucy estates, although its preserve is not distinctly named. It is, therefore, difficult to deny that a few herds of deer might have roamed, as at present, about Charlecote House. The law of Shakespeare's day (5 Eliz. cap. 21) punished deer-stealers with three months' imprisonment and the payment of thrice the amount of the damage done; but the popular opinion was on the side of the poacher. "Venison is nothing so sweet as when it is stolen," was a contemporary proverb.

In 1828 Sir Walter Scott was informed by the owner of Charlecote that Shakespeare stole the deer—not from Charlecote, but from Fulbroke Park. This version of the exploit was first promulgated about a century ago, and was very well received. The antiquary, Ireland, introduced into his *Views on the Warwickshire Avon* (1795) an engraving of an old farmhouse in the hamlet of Fulbroke, where, he asserted, Shakespeare was temporarily imprisoned after his arrest. An adjoining hovel was also described for some years as Shakespeare's "deer-barn"; but the site of these buildings (now removed) was not Sir Thomas Lucy's property in Elizabeth's reign, and the amended legend is a pure invention.

The ballad which Shakespeare is reported to have fastened on the park-gates of Charlecote does not survive. An old man, who lived in a village near Stratford and died in 1703 at the age of ninety, is stated to have repeated from memory the following lines, and they are often identified with the libel which irritated Sir Thomas Lucy:—

> A Parliament member, a justice of peace,
> At home a poor scarecrowe, at London an asse;
> If lowsie is Lucy, as some volke miscalle it,
> Then Lucy is lowsie, whatever befall it.
>   He thinks himself greate,
>   Yet an asse in his state,
>   We allowe by his ears but with asses to mate,
> If Lucy is lowsie, as some volke miscalle it,
> Then Lucy is lowsie whatever befall it.

Attempts have been made to prove the genuineness of this worthless effusion. That it is some two hundred years old may be admitted; the author is undoubtedly correct in describing Lucy as "a Parliament member and justice of peace," which may be urged as proof that he was not unacquainted with Lucy's biography, but that the lines are three centuries old, and the work of Shakespeare, may be safely denied.

Shakespeare undoubtedly took a subtle revenge. He immortalised Charlecote and its owner in the character of Justice Shallow. According to Davies, of Saperton, "his revenge was so great that he [*i.e.* Lucy] is his [*i.e.* Shakespeare's] Justice Clodpate, and [he] calls him a great man, and that, in allusion to his name, bore three louses rampant for his arms." Justice Shallow came to birth in the second part of Shakespeare's *Henry IV.* (written about 1597). He is, as all the world knows, a garrulous old gentleman, who is proud to call himself "one of the King's justices of the peace," and ostentatiously parades reminiscences of his wild days. His house is in Gloucestershire, and in the court before it Falstaff reviews, with the aid of the owner acting as commissioner of the muster, his far-famed ragged regiment. His hospitality and his officiousness as justice and muster-man tally with all that is known of Lucy, but the identity of the two does not distinctly appear until Shallow's entrance in the opening scene of the *Merry Wives of Windsor* (probably written early in 1598). There he has come from Gloucestershire to Windsor to "make a Star-chamber matter" of a poaching affray on his estates. Falstaff is the offender. In a rambling and querulous conversation with his cousin Slender, Shallow refers with pride to his ancient lineage, and Slender corroborates him with an allusion to "the dozen white *luces*," on his "old coat" of arms. This is undoubtedly a blundering jest on the arms of the Charlecote Lucys, described by heralds as "three *luces* hauriant argent." A *luce* is in modern English a pike —a fact that accounts for Falstaff's comparison elsewhere of Shallow to an "old pike." The three *luces*, or pikes, are engraved on all the monuments to the Lucys in Charlecote Church, and on one monument a quartering of their arms appears with three fish in each of four divisions. Thus Slender may not be talking altogether at random when he speaks of the dozen *luces*. Shakespeare distinctly emphasises the reference to the Lucy arms. "It is an old coat," says Shallow, in reply to Slender. "The dozen white louses do become an old coat well," is Sir Hugh Evans's punning comment, and the dialogue lingers about the topic. Later in the scene, as soon as Falstaff enters, Shallow abruptly introduces the business which has brought him from Gloucestershire. "Knight, you have beaten my men, killed my deer, and broke open my lodge!" is his charge; "But not kissed your keeper's daughter," is Falstaff's humorous rejoinder.

Shall.—Tut, a pin! this shall be answered.
Fal.—I will answer it straight. I have done all this; that is now answered.
Shall.—The Council shall know this.
Fal.—'Twere better for you if it were known in counsel [*i.e.* if you took good counsel about it]; you'll be laughed at.

And there the matter ends. Shallow and Lucy are in identical situations throughout. By many smaller details their identity could be illustrated. Lucy was an enthusiast for archery, according to an extant letter sent

Charlecote House

by him to Leicester; so was Justice Shallow. The reiterated mention of Shallow's judicial functions suggests the repeated exercise of Sir Thomas Lucy's legal authority, which is vouched for by the Stratford-on-Avon Corporation archives. Justice Shallow is, beyond reasonable doubt, Shakespeare's satiric sketch of the builder of Charlecote.[1]

[1] An admirably full and scholarly account of the Shakespearian traditions that have gathered about Charlecote is to be found in the *seventh* edition of Mr. J. O. Halliwell-Phillipps's *Outlines of the Life of Shakespeare*, vol. i. pp. 67-76, 157-161; and vol. ii. pp. 379-390.

ARMS OF LUCY.

XXI

INDOOR AMUSEMENTS

OF indoor amusements, few were probably in much vogue at Stratford. But cards seem to have been occasionally played.

In foul weather (says Vincent, a country gentleman, in the *Dialogue with an English Courtier*, 1586) we send for some honest neighbours, if haply we be with our wives alone at home (as seldom we are) and with them we play at Dice, and Cards, sorting ourselves according to the number of players, and their skill, some to Ticktack, some Lurch, some to Irish game, or Doublets: others sit close to the Cards, at Post, and Pair, at Ruff or Colchester Trump, at Mack or Maw: yea, there are some ever so fresh gamesters, as will bear you company at Novem Quinque, at Faring, Tray trip, or one-and-thirty, for I warrant you, we have right good fellows in the country; sometimes also (for shift of sports, you know, is delectable) we fall to Slide Thrift, to Penny prick, and in winter nights we use certain Christmas games very proper, and of much agility; we want not also pleasant mad-headed knaves, that be properly learned, and will read in diverse pleasant books and good

BIDFORD.

Authors; as Sir Guy of Warwick, the Four Sons of Aymon, the Ship of Fools, the Budget of Demands, the Hundred Merry Tales, the Book of Riddles, and many other excellent writers both witty and pleasant. These pretty and pithy matters do sometimes recreate our minds, chiefly after long sitting and loss of money.

But many preferred to recreate themselves in an alehouse, and play there an elementary form of bagatelle called "shovel-board." The Stratford people still tell how Shakespeare often crossed from New Place to the Falcon Tavern, on the opposite side of Chapel Street, and played this game with his neighbours, at the very board now preserved in the house at New Place; but, unluckily for the tradition, we know very well that the tavern sprang up at a later date, and in Shakespeare's day was a private dwelling-house in the occupation, early in the seventeenth century, of Mrs. Katharine Temple, and later of Joseph Boles, a friend of John Hall, the poet's son-in-law.

There is another very persistent tradition at Stratford, to show that Shakespeare frequently took his ease in an inn. According to this story, Shakespeare engaged, as a youth, in a famous drinking-match at another tavern called the Falcon, at Bidford, some five or six miles from his native town. The tale dates, in its most authentic form, from no earlier year than 1762. A gentleman visiting Stratford was then taken to Bidford, and shown "in the hedge a crab-tree called Shakespeare's Canopy, because under it our poet slept one night; for he, as well as Ben Jonson, loved a glass for the pleasure of society." Shakespeare (the story proceeds) "having heard much of the men of the village as deep drinkers and merry fellows, one day went over to Bidford to take a cup with them. He inquired of a shepherd for the Bidford drinkers, who replied that they were absent, but the sippers were at home, and, 'I suppose,' continued the sheep-keeper, 'they will be sufficient for you;' and so, indeed, they were;—he was forced to take up his lodgings under that tree for some hours."

This story has since been elaborated by Stratford writers, who make Shakespeare "extremely fond of drinking hearty draughts of English ale, and glorying in being thought a person of superior eminence in that profession," and assert that, being worsted in a drinking contest with the junior drinking club of the Sippers at Bidford, he, with his companions, slept under a crab-tree for a whole night. Shakespeare and his companions were next day invited to renew the contest, but the poet wisely declined, saying, "I have drank with

> Piping Pebworth, Dancing Marston,
> Haunted Hillborough, Hungry Grafton,
> Dadgeing Exhall, Papist Wixford,
> Beggarly Broom, and Drunken Bidford "—

"meaning, by this doggrel, with the bibulous competitors who had arrived from the first-named seven villages, all of which are within a few miles of Bidford," and thus not far from Stratford. The rhyme is very halting, and few of the villages are specially noted for the qualities indicated by the epithets. Bidford, although it now strives manfully to deserve the epithet bestowed on it in these lines, was reputed in 1605 and 1606, to have its alehouses in good order and its rogues punished. In 1613, however, one John Darlingie was "presented" there for "keeping ill rule in his house on the Sabbath in service time by selling of ale," and later in the century the alehouse-keepers were guilty of many irregularities. The room pointed out at Bidford as forming part of the Falcon Tavern where Shakespeare's match took place, and the antique chair at the Stratford birthplace stated to have belonged to the room, are relics of highly doubtful authenticity. Other versions of the tale make the drunken band sleep under the crab-tree "from Saturday night till the following Monday morning, when they were roused by workmen going to their labour." The crab-tree was still standing in the present century, but was removed in a decayed condition in 1824.

A similar legend represents Shakespeare as a frequenter of another village inn at Wincot, or Wilmecote, his mother's birthplace. This house (we are told) "was resorted to by Shakespeare for the sake of diverting himself with a fool who belonged to a neighbouring mill." "Marian Hackett, the fat ale-wife of Wincot," has been identified with the "genial hostess" of this inn, and Stephen Sly, one of her customers in the *Taming of the Shrew*, was undoubtedly the name of a resident at Stratford who is sometimes described in the records as a labourer and sometimes as servant to William Combe. Perhaps at this tavern, too, old John Naps, Peter Turf, and Henry Pimpernell held revelry. The references in the *Taming of the Shrew*

HILLBOROUGH.

to Wincot were well understood locally. Sir
Aston Cokain, addressing a poem in 1658 to Mr.
Clement Fisher, of Wincot, reminded him how

> Shakespeare your Wincot ale hath much renownd,
> That foxd a beggar so (by chance was found
> Sleeping) that there needed not many a word
> To make him to believe he was a lord.

The far-famed beggar, Kit Sly, was doubtless a Stratford character; he was probably related to the Stephen Sly to whom reference has just been made, and to Joan Sly, who in 1630 was fined by the Stratford magistrates for breaking the Sabbath by travelling.

A quart of ale was a dish for a king all over England in Elizabethan days, and there is nothing more probable, although the proof must remain for ever incomplete, than that Shakespeare indulged in alehouse festivities. The sober magistrates of Stratford did the same. They always celebrated the visits of neighbouring gentry at quarter sessions by deep potations. Whenever Sir Thomas Lucy visited Stratford, a pottle of wine and a quartern of sugar, or a quart of burnt sack and sugar, were placed at his disposal either at the Swan or the Bear, or at one of the aldermen's private houses. Sir

Edward Greville, the moat of whose manor-house at Milcote is still visible in the fields there, came very often to the town at the close of the sixteenth century to be entertained at a municipal banquet, and to quaff his quart of sack and gallon of claret. His more famous relative, the poet, Sir Fulk Greville, also came over from Beauchamp's Court by Warwick to take wine, sugar, and cakes with the magistrates. He or Sir Edward or Sir Thomas Lucy would send them a buck or doe to form the substance of their meal together, and would sometimes accept a sugar-loaf or a keg of sturgeon instead of wine. When the itinerant justices visited the town, or the muster of the trained bands of the district was held there, the town council was not sparing in its gifts of sack and claret or Rhenish wine. At one of these entertainments sixteenpence was spent in wine and a penny in bread—a collocation of items which reminds one of the monstrous "halfpennyworth of bread to this intolerable deal of sack." None the less, these aldermen and burgesses of Stratford were ready next morning to set a poor artificer in the stocks for three days and three nights on the charge of wasting time in an alehouse.

XXII

CHRISTENINGS AND MARRIAGES

OTHER kinds of merrymaking celebrated the happy crises of domestic life. The christening of a child was a time of festival and gift-giving. Apostle-spoons were always bestowed on the infant among the middle classes, as silver and gold cups were bestowed among the upper. After baptism at the church font the child was wrapped in a chrisome, or white chrism-cloth; and Dame Quickly refers to the practice when she compares Falstaff on his deathbed to "any christom child." Shakespeare must have often seen such ceremonies. His sister Joan, who afterwards married William Hart, of Stratford, was baptized when he was five years old; his sister Anna, who died at the age of eight, when he was seven; his brothers Richard and Edmund, when he was ten and sixteen respectively. His eldest daughter, Susanna, was baptized in the parish church, 26th May 1583, and his twin children, Hamnet and Judith, 2d February 1585. Nor does this exhaust the list of christenings which he attended. The nephew of Sir Roger Lestrange vouched for the

STRATFORD, FROM THE SOUTH-EAST.

story that Shakespeare was godfather to a son of Ben Jonson's, and gave him a dozen good *latin* (*i.e.* brass) spoons, for his father, as he said jestingly, to translate.

But weddings formed the chief events in the domestic annals of Elizabethan merriment. There were first the espousals to be celebrated —the public announcement of betrothal. The clergyman directed this important ceremony in the house of the bride's parents, and it was often regarded in the country as equivalent to a marriage. Shakespeare describes its details in *Twelfth Night* as

> A contract of eternal bond of love,
> Confirm'd by mutual joinder of your hands,
> Attested by the holy close of lips,
> Strengthen'd by interchangement of your rings:

and sealed finally by the testimony of the priest. The lady usually received from her lover a bent sixpence, or gloves, with handkerchiefs and fruit. The marriage ceremony followed at varying intervals. At the simplest weddings the bride was led to church in her best gown, with her hair hanging down her back, by boys "with bride laces and rosemary tied about their silken sleeves." A bride cup filled with wine and decorated with rosemary and silk ribbons was borne before her. Musicians and girls followed her, one of whom carried the bridal cake. The bridal cup appears from the account of Petruchio's wedding in the *Taming of the Shrew* to have been drunk in the church.

A full account of a Warwickshire "bride-ale," as the wedding was called, is given in the description of the Queen's visit to Kenilworth, when she graced one with her presence. Doubtless, Mary Arden was married to John Shakespeare at Wilmecote in 1557 with such ceremony as this. First came sixteen lusty lads and bold bachelors of the parish on horseback, two by two, with blue buckram bride laces and branches of green broom (because rosemary was scanty) on their left arms, and sticks of eldertree in their right. Among them was the bridegroom in a tawny worsted jacket, "a fair straw hat with a capital crown, steeplewise upon his head," and a pair of harvest gloves in his hand. After this band came morris dancers and three fair girls. A country bumpkin followed them with the bride cup; behind him walked the bride between two ancient parishioners, honest men, and she was accompanied by twenty-four damsels as bridesmaids.

Shakespeare's own marriage with Anne Hathaway, of Shottery, a mile from Stratford, was probably less ceremonious. Both his and her parents disapproved of it, and there was certainly an awkward disparity of age between them, he being but eighteen and she twenty-six. According to tradition, the marriage took place

ANNE HATHAWAY'S COTTAGE AT SHOTTERY. INTERIOR.

at Luddington, in a church which has now disappeared, and of which the schoolmaster, Thomas Hunt, was curate. The license, or "bond against impediments," preserved in the Worcester registry, is dated 28th November 1582. Two respectable husbandmen of Shottery, Falk Sandells and John Richardson, attest it. But espousals had doubtless been quietly solemnised earlier, and Anne Hathaway had then been betrothed to Shakespeare as his wife. Their first child was born in May 1583.

There is an account extant of the celebration of a precontract, under similarly unprepossessing circumstances, at Alcester in 1588, where the contract took the place of a more regular marriage. The lady was present without any friends, and explained their absence by the statement that she thought she could not obtain her mother's goodwill, but nevertheless, quoth she, "I am the same woman that I was before." Her lover merely asked her "whether she was content to betake herself unto him, and she answered, offering her hand, which he also took upon the offer that she was content by her troth, and 'thereto,' said she, 'I give thee my faith and before these witnessess, that I am thy wife,' and then he likewise answered in these words, viz. 'And I give thee my faith and troth, and become thy husband.'" This was doubtless the form that Shakespeare's betrothal took, and, although not very irregular for those days, certainly caused many of his youthful embarrassments.

Richard Hathaway's cottage at Shottery, reached from Stratford by open paths across wide meadows, is still standing, and an ancient chair by the chimney corner and bacon cupboard in the parlour is called "Shakespeare's courting chair." The house is encircled by an old-fashioned flower and kitchen garden, and forms a picturesque relic of Elizabethan country life. Attempts have been made, with doubtful success, to detect resemblances to it in Celia's description of the cottage which she and Rosalind occupy in the Forest of Arden. The Hathaways had been small farmers at Shottery before the middle of the sixteenth century, and there were branches of the family settled at Stratford. In 1580, another Anne Hathaway had married Alderman Wilson there, and a Thomas Hathaway, son of Margaret Hathaway, died at Stratford in 1601. There

ANNE HATHAWAY'S COTTAGE AT SHOTTERY.

is evidence to prove that Richard Hathaway, Anne's father, who died in 1582, in the same year as Anne married, was, early in Elizabeth's reign, on friendly terms with John Shakespeare, and it is probable that the poet met Anne at his father's house for the first time. That he had an affection for her quiet native village is shown by the fact that in 1598 he contemplated the purchase there of "some odd yard-land." Probably the Richard Hathway, or Hathaway, who takes his place in the lower ranks of the dramatists of London early in the next century, was a near relative of the great dramatist's wife.

OLD CHURCH OF LUDDINGTON.

XXIII

SHAKESPEARE AT STRATFORD IN LATER LIFE

It is no part of my present plan to trace the progressive career of Shakespeare as a dramatist. His life at Stratford as the woolstapler's son who "went to London very meanly, and came in time to be exceeding wealthy," is alone to be noted here. Nor will it be necessary to follow him in his journeyings to and fro the metropolis. His first journey was doubtless made in the covered waggon of the carrier who made weekly journeys, or on foot, but later he doubtless travelled on horseback. It was a common practice to hire horses for travelling at twelvepence the first day, and eightpence a day afterwards, until they were returned to the owner; but Shakespeare could have afforded long before his death to ride a horse of his own.

There were two routes between Stratford and London—one by Oxford and High Wycombe, through Shipston-on-Stour, Chipping Norton, Woodstock, the Chilterns, Beaconsfield, Hillingdon Hill, Hanwell, Acton, and Kensington; the other by Banbury and Aylesbury.[1] Tradition points to the former route as Shakespeare's favourite road, and signalises the Crown Inn, near Carfax, at Oxford, as one of his resting-places, where he found "witty company" and a fair hostess with whom scandal will have it he made too free. Aubrey asserts that at Grendon, near Oxford, "he happened to take the humour of the constable in *Midsummer Night's Dream*"—by which he meant, we may suppose, *Much Ado about Nothing*—but there were watchmen of the Dogberry type all over England, and probably at Stratford itself. Lord Burghley, writing to Walsingham in 1586, described how on a long journey he saw the watch at every town's end standing with long staves under alehouse pentices, and how at Enfield they declared they were watching for

[1] For an interesting account of the journey by road from Stratford to London see Professor J. W. Hales's *Notes and Essays on Shakespeare* (1884), pp. 1-24.

three young men, whom they would surely know because "one of the parties hath a hooked nose"—a statement upon which Burghley makes the prudent comment that "if they be no better instructed but to find three persons by one of them having a hooked nose, they may miss thereof." The inns all along the Elizabethan country roads were famed for their comfort. "The world affords," writes one traveller, Fynes Morison, "not such inns as England hath either for good and cheap entertainment after the guests' own pleasure, or for humble attendance on passengers; yea, even in very poor villages." The host and hostess and the servants zealously attended to the needs of horse and man. What was left over from a guest's supper was carefully preserved for his breakfast, his chamber was kept well cleaned and warmed, and a few pence was all that was expected by the chamberlain and ostler when the traveller left to pursue his journey. Up to the very last years of his life, Shakespeare paid frequent visits to London, and very often must he have hasted to his bed "with travel tired" at an hospitable roadside inn.

When Shakespeare left Stratford-on-Avon in

1585, his wife and three children remained behind, but at no period is it probable that he was long separated from them. His fellow-townsmen at all times knew of his worldly prosperity, and were conscious of a desire on his part to stand well with them. Abraham Sturley, who was once bailiff, writing apparently to a brother early in 1598, says: "This is one special remembrance from our father's motion. It seemeth by him that our countryman, Mr. Shakspere, is willing to disburse some money upon some odd yardland or other at Shottery, or near about us: he thinketh it a very fit pattern to move him to deal in the matter of our tithes. By the instructions you can give him thereof, and by the friends he can make therefore, we think it a fair mark for him to shoot at, and would do us much good." To Richard Quiney, the father of Thomas Quiney, afterwards Shakespeare's son-in-law, who was staying in 1598 at the Bell, in Carter Lane, London, and endeavouring to relieve the town of the payment of a subsidy, Abraham Sturley also wrote, on 4th November 1598, that since the town was wholly unable, in consequence of the terrible dearth of corn ("beyond all other countries that I can hear of dear and over dear"), to pay the national taxes, he hoped "that our countryman Mr. Wm. Shak. would procure us money, which I will like of, as I shall hear when, and where, and how." Richard Quiney was himself harassed by debt, and had just before (25th October) addressed a like request to Shakespeare in his own behalf. "Loving countryman," the application ran—and the manuscript, which is still extant, is the only surviving paper besides his will known to have been pressed by Shakespeare's own hands—"Loving countryman, I am bold of you as of a friend, craving your help with xxx*li*. . . . You shall friend me much in helping me out of all the debts I owe in London, I thank God, and much quiet my mind, which would not be indebted. . . ."

Shakespeare apparently maintained very good relations with his father, and the coat-of-arms granted to John Shakespeare in 1596 was undoubtedly the result of his son's exertions. John's own fortunes had long continued to decline. In 1587 an importunate creditor, Nicholas Lane, had made an attempt to distrain on his goods, but found none on which

APPROACH TO SHOTTERY, FROM STRATFORD.

he could lay hands. John had already in 1579 mortgaged his estate of Ashbies at Wilmecote for forty pounds to Edmund Lambert, a family friend, and sold in 1579 some of his property at Snitterfield to Robert Webbe, yeoman, for four pounds. A vexatious lawsuit arose out of the mortgage of Ashbies. John Shakespeare, although hard pressed by other debts, offered in 1580, according to the agreement, to pay off the mortgage, but Lambert refused to relinquish the property. On his death in 1597 his son continued in possession, and John Shakespeare endeavoured to deprive him, with what success is not known. In 1592 John Shakespeare was in worse plight: he was returned as a "recusant." Commissioners had come to Stratford to enforce the penalty of twenty pounds to which those who did not attend church once a month were liable. The appearance of Shakespeare's name in the list of defaulters has suggested that he was a Roman Catholic. But it was not merely a man's religious opinions that kept him from church. The statute acknowledged the lawfulness of pleading in excuse not only "age, sickness, and impotency of body," but fear of creditors. It was doubtless under the last disability that John Shakespeare suffered. But throughout this troubled time he still lived in the old house in Henley Street; and although he is said to have let out an adjoining tenement, he never parted with the copyhold of the property. In 1601 he died intestate, and William doubtless followed him to the grave. The poet, as the eldest son, inherited the houses in Henley Street, but his mother continued to live there till her death in September 1608.

Five years before his father's death, another and a far sadder funeral had brought Shakespeare to Stratford. On 11th August 1596 there was buried in the parish church his only son, Hamnet, aged eleven. That loss must have tempered the satisfaction with which the creator of Arthur and Mamillius witnessed the triumphant success that attended the production at the same date of his *Romeo and Juliet*. It was in the next year (1597) that he made his first purchase of landed property at Stratford, and bought the great house of New Place, with two barns and two gardens. For it he paid sixty pounds to William Underhill, gentleman, who had succeeded Alderman

Bott in 1567 in its ownership. In May 1602 the poet purchased one hundred and seven acres of land to the north-east of the town, from the Combes, his wealthy neighbours; and on 28th September following he bought a cottage of one Walter Getley, adjoining his garden in Chapel Lane. In July 1605 he added largely to these properties by buying for £440, "the unexpired term of a moiety of the interest in a lease granted in 1554 for ninety-two years of the tithes of Stratford, Bishopston, and Welcombe, subject to certain annual payments." This was the last of the poet's Stratford purchases of real estate, all of which were completed before he was forty-two years old.

There is further evidence that he occasionally traded in agricultural produce, as his father had done before him. In 1598 few of his neighbours owned more grain than he. Between March and May 1604 he sold one pound nineteen shillings and tenpence worth of malt to one Philip Rogers, and lent him two shillings afterwards: six shillings of the debt were repaid, but Shakespeare had to bring an action in the local court to recover the balance. The records of 1608 and 1609 show Shakespeare engaged in recovering another debt of six pounds from John Addenbroke. Shakespeare gained a verdict, but Addenbroke decamped, and made the success a barren one. But at that period Shakespeare was one of the richest men in the town.

During these years Shakespeare was frequently passing to and from London, and while at Stratford he does not always seem to have resided at New Place. He rebuilt it, apparently of stone, in 1598, soon after purchasing it, and planted an orchard in the garden, of which the mulberry tree—planted about 1609—was long a famous survival. Early in the seventeenth century the town-clerk, Thomas Greene, who claimed to be Shakespeare's cousin, lived in the house, but he removed about 1609. It has been suggested that between 1598 and 1607 Shakespeare and his family lived with his mother in the houses in Henley Street, which his father's death in 1601 had placed in his hands. In 1607 his eldest daughter, Susannah, married John Hall, a rising physician of puritan tendencies, recently settled in Stratford, who purchased a large house in Old Town. And it was there, according to some conjectures, that Shakespeare took up a temporary residence between 1607 and 1609. After the latter date, New Place was his permanent home, and he rarely left Stratford in subsequent years. He had many friends there. Old John Combe, of whose suspected usury he laughingly disapproved, was living at the college. He saw much of the Quineys, his father's and his own acquaintances from youth. The second house from New Place, a very substantial building which is still standing, was inhabited by Julius Shaw, who dealt regularly in wool, corn, and malt, and occasionally in wood and tiles. Shaw was a member of the town council in 1603, a chamberlain in 1609, an alderman in 1613, and bailiff in 1616. Shakespeare knew him well, and called him in just before his death to witness his will. Relatives were also numerous in the neighbourhood. The house in Henley Street Shakespeare appears to have let (after his final removal to New Place) to his sister Joan and her husband, William Hart, who is described as a hatter. (There they brought up their three sons, the poet's nephews: William, born in 1600, Thomas, born in 1605, and Michael, born in 1608; and the occupiers of the house in the early years of the present century claimed descent from the Harts.) Shakespeare's brothers, Gilbert, three years his junior, and Richard, ten years his junior, lived at Stratford, and the former assisted him to complete some of his purchases of land.

Visitors to Stratford doubtless knew the wealthy inhabitant of New Place. Old Sir Thomas Lucy had died at Charlecote, 7th July 1600, and his son and heir died three years later. But a third Sir Thomas Lucy, grandson of Shakespeare's early enemy, was diligent in the discharge of local judicial functions. In early life he had travelled on the continent with Lord Herbert of Cherbury, and was apparently a man of culture. He was often to be seen riding about Stratford. We know that in 1632 he conferred with Shakespeare's son-in-law, John Hall, on local business, and afterwards refreshed himself at the Swan Inn. There is every reason to assume that he and the poet were known to each other. As much may be said of another great neighbour — Sir Fulk Greville of Alcester and of Beauchamp's Court,

CLIFFORD CHURCH AND OLD HOUSES.

Warwick, a poet, a statesman, and the friend in earlier days of Sir Philip Sidney. A more congenial acquaintance was Michael Drayton, a native of Warwick and an ardent lover of the county of his birth.

Shakespeare never coveted municipal office; he was content to be merely Mr. Shakespeare, gentleman, of Stratford, and neither alderman nor bailiff. There is little reason to suspect that the cause of his neglect of this road to local fame is to be ascribed to any contempt on his part for its humble worth. It was due rather to the puritan atmosphere which was fast settling upon Stratford when he was in a position to avail himself of municipal honours. His father had evinced puritan leanings, with which his son was clearly never in sympathy. As early as 1564, when John Shakespeare was chamberlain, he paid two shillings "for defacing image in chapel." But it was some years before the puritan spirit laid a firm enough hold on the town council to induce them, as they did on two occasions in the early part of the seventeenth century, to consider "the inconvenience of plays." Shakespeare must have felt some amusement when the news was brought him from the council chamber, opposite New Place, that after very serious consideration the council resolved, on 7th February 1612, that plays were unlawful, and "the sufferance of them against the orders heretofore made, and against the example of other well-governed cities and boroughs"; and the council was therefore "content," the resolution ran, "and they conclude that the penalty of x*s*. imposed [on players] be x*li.* henceforth." Ten years later the king's players were bribed by the council to leave the city without playing. The drinking of sack and claret by the burgesses did not cease, however, but it, too, was now directed to advance soberer causes than of old. The council began to invite puritan preachers to preach in the town and to take their pottle of wine and quart of sack, at the municipal expense, after the sermon. One of these incongruous entertainments was, singularly enough, celebrated in 1614 at Shakespeare's own house. "One quart of sack and one quart of claret wine given to the preacher at New Place" is an item in the chamberlain's accounts for 1614. It was probably John Hall, the poet's son-in-law, who organised that gathering; or it may be that the preacher was personally attractive, and that the owner of New Place was anxious to make his acquaintance. Shakespeare, it should also be remembered, must have been a regular attendant at the parish church, and may at times have enjoyed a sermon. The pew which the residents at New Place occupied, called from its early owners the Clopton Pew, was near the pulpit, on the south side of the nave.

XXIV

THE GUNPOWDER PLOT—COMBE'S DEATH—THE ATTEMPT TO ENCLOSE THE WELCOMBE FIELDS

Some stirring episodes disturbed Stratford in the dramatist's last days. In 1598 there were riots, owing to the famine; in 1602 "rogues were taken at Clifford," amid much unexplained excitement, finally quelled by draughts of sack and Rhenish wine given to the townsmen at the municipal expense. In 1605 and 1606 much consternation was caused in the neighbourhood by the Gunpowder Plot. Some of the leading conspirators lived near Stratford. At Clopton House, then the property of Baron Carew, William Clopton's son-in-law, lived Ambrose Rookwood, a chief abettor of the plot, and he received there many of his associates. Catesby lived near Lapworth. When the plot was discovered, the bailiff of

THE CLOPTON PEW.

T

Stratford was ordered to make an inventory of Rookwood's goods. He and many burgesses proceeded to Clopton House on 26th February 1606, and found much Papist paraphernalia, which they duly seized.[1]

Eight years later, on 10th July 1614, old John Combe of the College died, and was buried in the parish church with much ceremony. Some while before his death, he had told Shakespeare, according to a well-known story of little authenticity, that he believed the poet intended to write his epitaph, and begged him to tell him what he would say of him. Shakespeare replied with four lines, the sharpness of whose satire on Combe's 10 per cent loans is said to have brought the friendship of the two to an end—

> Ten in the hundred lies here engraved,
> 'Tis a hundred to ten his soul is not saved.
> If any man ask, Who lies in this tomb?
> Oh! oh! quoth the devil, 'tis my John-a-Combe.

As a matter of fact, Combe's tomb bore an inscription recording his many charitable bequests to the poor of Stratford, and by his will he left five pounds to "Mr. William

---

[1] *Cf.* Professor Hales's *Notes, etc., on Shakespeare*, pp. 25-56.

Shackspere." Other bequests prove Combe to have lived on intimate terms with all the

MEMORIAL OF SIR HENRY RAINFORD IN CLIFFORD CHURCH.

neighbouring gentry, including Sir Henry Rainford, whose elaborate monument stands still in Clifford Church.

Combe was a favourable specimen of the new class of country landowners which the development of commerce had made numerous throughout sixteenth century England. His chief object in life was to secure a fortune, but he sought at the same time to stand well with his neighbours, especially with those in high social station. Speculation in land offered a ready means of attaining his two aims of wealth and social dignity. Land (as we have already noted [1]) was in those days an investment which could ensure a profit, but for this purpose it was necessary to apply it chiefly to grazing uses, and to secure wide areas. The agricultural labourer suffered under such masters. Little labour was required, and the agricultural population dwindled. A greed for great estates invariably characterised the new class of landowners. Small owners were absorbed by large ones, and lands held in common by municipal corporations were constantly threatened with enclosure. If old John Combe did not himself exemplify the worst vices of the new system, he could not avoid inflicting some hardship on his poorer neigh-

[1] See pp. 115-116.

bours; and his son and successor, William Combe, had far less consideration than his father for either the tillers of the soil or the townsmen of Stratford as owners of the common fields near his estates. Shakespeare certainly bore in mind the grievances of the South Warwickshire peasants when he made Corin, the shepherd of the Forest of Arden, in his *As You Like It*, complain—

> But I am shepherd to another man,
> And do not shear the fleeces that I graze.
> My master is of churlish disposition,
> And little recks to find the way to heaven
> By doing deeds of hospitality.

The evil influence of "the greedy gentlemen which are sheepmongers and graziers," and are worse than "the caterpillars and locusts of Egypt," is a commonplace in the charges brought by those who under Elizabeth denounced the vices of the age. "They have depopulated and overthrown whole towns, and made thereof sheep pastures nothing profitable to the commonwealth," is the opening phrase of "a petition of the Diggers of Warwickshire" addressed "to all other diggers" in the reign of James I.

The enclosure of the common fields attached to villages and towns was repeatedly attempted by the new landowners in the face of many prohibitory enactments, and often with complete success. This pillage of valued rights was always hotly resented, and often violently resisted. In May and June 1607 the peasantry of the midland counties, smarting under many such invasions of their privileges and properties, were involved in something like a rebellion. "People," the proclamation issued to repress the disturbances ran, "did assemble themselves in riotous and tumultuous manner, sometimes in the night and sometimes in the day, under pretence of laying open enclosed grounds of late years taken in to their domage, as they say." In Warwickshire and elsewhere, says Stow, "a great number of common persons . . . violently cut and broke down hedges . . . and laid open all such enclosures of commons and other grounds as they found enclosed."[1] At Hill's Norton, in Warwickshire, the insurgents assembled to the number of 3000, armed with spades, shovels, bills, and pikes. The leader, John Reynolds, was called Captain

[1] Stow's *Chronicles* (1632), p. 890.

Pouch, because he pretended that a pouch which he was in the habit of wearing contained enough to feed any number of rebels. On subsequent examination there was only found in the pouch "a piece of green cheese." Reynolds or Pouch asserted that he had authority from the king to overthrow enclosures. But when the agitators declined to disperse on the issue of a proclamation promising an investigation into their grievances, military force was employed, and all the ringleaders were arrested and hanged. James I. expressed himself strongly against the enclosures, and admitted the injury thus wrought on the poor labourers.

After such disturbances in the peaceful neighbourhood of Stratford, it is surprising to find that William, John Combe's heir, had no sooner succeeded to his father's lands than he attempted to enclose the common fields about his estate at Welcombe, which undoubtedly belonged to the Stratford townsmen. In the autumn the corporation of Stratford first became aware of Combe's intention, and they resolved to offer it the sternest resistance.

Shakespeare had some personal interest in the matter. He owned some neighbouring lands as well as part of the tithes of the threatened fields. But he had small sympathy with popular rights, and when Combe's agent, Replingham, in October 1614 formally drew up a deed engaging that he should suffer no injury by the enclosure, he threw his influence into Combe's scale.

In November 1614 he was in London, and Thomas Greene, town clerk of Stratford-on-Avon, who calls Shakespeare his cousin, although it is improbable that they were relatives, visited him there to discuss the position of affairs.

On 23d December 1614 the corporation assembled in formal meeting and drew up a letter to Shakespeare imploring him to aid them in the struggle. Greene himself sent to the dramatist "a note of inconveniences [that] would happen by the enclosure." But although an ambiguous entry [1] of a later date (September 1615),

[1] The words are "Sept. Mr. Shakspeare tellyng J. Greene that I was not able to beare the encloseing of Welcombe." J. Greene is to be distinguished from Thomas Greene the diarist. The entry therefore implies that Shakespeare told J. Greene that the writer of the diary, Thomas Greene, was not able to bear the enclosure. Dr. C. M. Ingleby published in 1885 a careful facsimile of the extant pages of Green's diary (now preserved at Stratford) with a transcript by Mr. E. J. L. Scott of the British Museum. Mr. Scott showed that Greene's writing of this entry can only be read as we give it. Those who wish

in the few extant pages of Greene's ungrammatical diary has been tortured into an expression of disgust on Shakespeare's part at Combe's conduct, it is quite clear that Shakespeare adhered to his agreement with Combe's agent, and tacitly supported him. Happily Combe failed. The corporation carried their case into the law courts, and the decision was in their favour. It is interesting to note that one of the disputed parcels of land, called then as now "the Dingles," is still unenclosed and offers the wayfarer an admirable point of view from which to survey Stratford and the neighbouring country.

to make Shakespeare a champion of popular rights unjustifiably interpret the "I" in "I was not able, etc." as "he,"—in which case Shakespeare would have told Greene that he (*i.e.* himself) disliked the enclosure. But all the correspondence addressed to Shakespeare on the subject by the council makes it clear that he and they took opposite views throughout.

XXV

SHAKESPEARE'S DEATH AND HIS DESCENDANTS

But before this dispute had reached its final settlement, Shakespeare's days came to a sudden close. He had welcomed the birth of his first grandchild, Elizabeth Hall, in 1608, the year of his mother's death. On 10th February 1616 there took place the marriage of his second daughter, Judith, who was then thirty-one years old, to the son of Richard Quiney, of High Street, Thomas Quiney, who was four years her junior. The ceremony was performed without a license, and some doubts as to its legality were subsequently raised. On 17th April the funeral of his brother-in-law, William Hart, the hatter, brought almost all the members of the family to the parish church. But it is doubtful if Shakespeare was present.

A few days before, according to an ancient

tradition, the poet was entertaining at New Place his two friends, Michael Drayton and Ben Jonson, and in the midst of the festivities was himself taken suddenly ill. Certain it is that on Tuesday, 23d April, six days after Hart's burial, Shakespeare died, at the age of fifty-two. On Thursday, 25th April, he was buried near the northern wall of the chancel, by the door of the charnel-house, where the bones dug up from the churchyard were deposited. The poet, fearful that his bones should suffer this indignity, is said to have written for inscription on his tomb—

> Good friend, for Jesus' sake forbeare
> To dig the dust enclosed heare;
> Bleste be the man that spares these stones,
> And curst be he that moves my bones.

According to the letter of one William Hall, a visitor to Stratford in 1694, recently brought to light, these verses were penned to suit "the capacity of clerks and sextons, for the most part a very ignorant set of people"; had this curse not threatened them, Hall proceeds, they would not have hesitated in course of time to remove Shakespeare's dust to "the bone-house," where waggon-loads of bones were

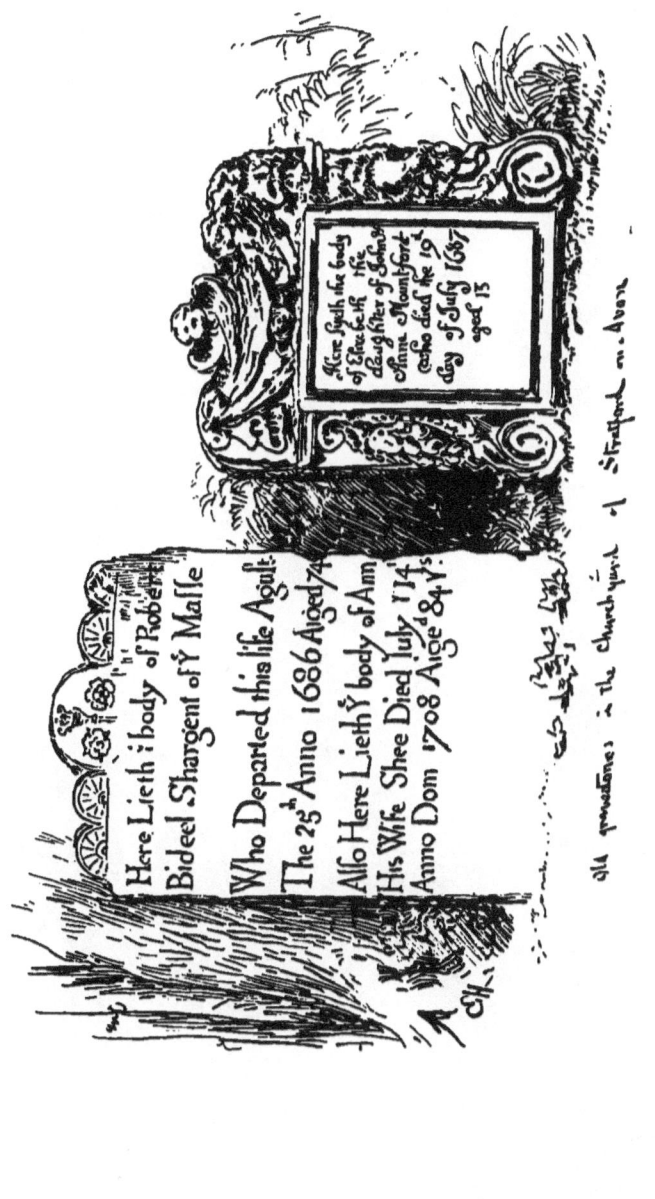

allowed to accumulate. The design, says the same authority, did not miss of its effect, for the grave was made seventeen feet deep, and was never opened, even to receive his wife, although she had expressed her desire to be buried with her husband.

Thus Stratford was deprived of the inhabitant to whose "wit" its renown is due. The burgesses of 1616 gave no sign that they were conscious that death was taking from them one who left anything besides a substantial worldly fortune to invite their respect. The great bell of the church was tolled, the bailiff and aldermen joined the funeral procession, rosemary was freely strewn above the grave, and a liberal banquet was provided for the mourners. Every honour was paid by the poet's fellow-townsmen, but none of those who were his daily companions at Stratford guessed that he had already gained an immortal fame for work done outside their parish boundaries.

Shakespeare's will, the first draft of which was drawn up in the January before his death, and the final draft by his bedside, was proved by Hall, in London, on the 22d of June. To his younger daughter, Judith, besides a portion of his landed property, he left £150, of which £100 was her marriage portion, and another £150 to be paid to her if alive three years after the date of the will. To his sister, Joan Hart, who had just become a widow, he left, besides a contingent reversionary interest in Judith's legacy, his wearing apparel, £20 in money, a life interest in the Henley Street property, and £5 to each of her three sons. To his granddaughter, Elizabeth Hall, he bequeathed his plate, with the exception of his broad silver and gilt bowl, which was reserved for Judith Quiney. To the poor of Stratford he gave £10; to Mr. Thomas Combe (apparently a brother of John, of the enclosure controversy) his sword; and to a number of Stratford friends, and to his "fellows," his partners in his theatrical speculations; John Hemyngs, Richard Burbage, and Henry Cundell, xxvj$s.$ viij$d.$ each, with which to buy memorial rings. To Susannah Hall, his elder daughter, he left, with remainder to her issue, New Place, almost all his land, barns, and gardens, and a house at Blackfriars, London. To his wife he gave only his second best bed with its furniture; all the rest of his household stuff passed to John Hall and his wife Susannah.

SHAKESPEARE'S MONUMENT.

The executors were Thomas Russell "esquier," and Francis Collins, a solicitor of Warwick. That the second best bed should have been bestowed on his wife was, according to contemporary notions, a mark of esteem, but that it should form the only bequest forms a strong argument in favour of the theory that the dramatist was not happy in his domestic life. His daughter Susannah was, according to his will, to take his wife's position as mistress of New Place.

Soon after his death, certainly before 1623, an elaborate monument was erected to Shakespeare's memory in the chancel of the parish church. The services of a London sculptor and tomb-maker, Gerard Johnson, son of a native of Amsterdam, with a shop near St. Saviour's Church, Southwark, not far from the Globe Theatre, were called into requisition, and the inscription was apparently written by a London friend of the dramatist. The bust above the inscribed tablet is probably from a cast taken after death, and, though scarcely pleasing, is the most authentic memorial of the poet's features. The words run—

*Judicio Pylium, genio Socratem, arte Maronem,
Terra tegit, populus maeret, Olympus habet.*

Stay, passenger, why goest thou by so fast?
Read, if thou canst, whom envious death hath plast
Within this monument; Shakspeare, with whome
Quick nature dide; whose name doth deck ys tombe
Far more then cost; sith all yt he hath writt
Leaves living art but page to serve his witt.

Obiit ano. doi. 1616. *Aetatis* 53. *Die* 23 *Ap.*

Of Shakespeare's family, his wife died on 6th August 1623, and was buried near her husband two days later. The Halls moved to New Place soon after the poet's death. John Hall increased his medical practice largely there, and his patients included the neighbouring gentry within a circuit of thirty miles. His puritanism grew more confirmed and precise in later life, and he frequently quarrelled with his neighbours. He was buried in the chancel of the parish church on the 25th November 1635. His only child had been since 1626 the wife of Thomas Nash, and to his son-in-law Hall bequeathed by will "his study of books." This study, it has been reasonably conjectured, must have formed the library of his father-in-law. The books do not appear to have been quickly

CHANCEL OF THE CHURCH OF THE HOLY TRINITY, STRATFORD.

removed from New Place, as his widow, who was still residing there, showed them in 1642 to James Cooke, a doctor professionally engaged at Stratford in the Civil War. He informed her that some manuscripts of her husband were among them, and offered to buy them of her, but this offer she declined, and disputed his opinion as to the authorship of the papers. Is it possible that some of her father's manuscripts were among them, or that she believed them to be? In any case, the information would have availed her little, for reading was not one of her accomplishments. Unhappily, nothing is known of the later history of the papers. Mistress Hall died on 11th July 1649, and was buried near her husband. Her tomb bears the epitaph—

> Witty above her sexe, but that's not all,
> Wise to salvation was good Mistris Hall;
> Something of Shakespere was in that, but this
> Wholy of Him with whom she's now in blisse.
> Then, Passenger, ha'st ne're a teare
>   To weepe with her that wept with all;—
> That wept, yet set herselfe to chere
>   Them up with comforts cordiall?
> Her love shall live, her mercy spread,
> When thou ha'st ne're a teare to shed.

Judith, Shakespeare's younger daughter, lived on till 9th February 1662. Her husband, soon after their marriage, removed to the house called the Cage, in Bridge Street, and was in business there as a vintner. He was a member of the town council from 1617 till 1630, when he fell into evil habits, and was fined for swearing and encouraging tipplers. From that date his fortunes declined. He finally sought employment in London, and died there about 1652. Judith's married life was thus not a very happy one. Of her three sons, the eldest, named Shakespeare, died in infancy, and the other two on reaching manhood, and she lived lonely at Stratford till death. The last surviving descendant of Shakespeare was his granddaughter Elizabeth Hall, whose first husband, Thomas Nash, a resident at Stratford, a student of Lincoln's Inn, died in 1647. She married afterwards Sir John Barnard, a Northamptonshire gentleman, and died, without issue by either marriage, in 1670. With her second husband she lived for some years at New Place, which she inherited from her mother, but she subsequently resided at Sir John's house at Abington, in Northamptonshire, and

in the church there she was buried. New Place she bequeathed to Sir John Barnard, and soon after his death, in 1674, it was repurchased by the Clopton family.

It is unnecessary to pursue the history of Stratford beyond these points. Of the final fortunes of New Place, it only remains to tell of its rebuilding by a Hugh Clopton in 1703, before any authentic pictorial representation of its appearance in Shakespeare's day had been made, and of its ultimate demolition in 1759 by Francis Gastrell, Vicar of Stratford, to avoid the pertinacity of sightseers and the payment of local taxes. Of other structural changes that Stratford underwent in the last century, the chief were the destruction of the College and the erection of the Townhall. To the new Townhall the municipal offices were transferred, and the ancient Guildhall was thus left untenanted. The general historian treats of the part played by the town in the civil warfare of the seventeenth century, of the story of Queen Henrietta Maria's flying visit to New Place in 1643, and of the quartering of soldiers at the time in Shakespeare's dwelling-place. The legal antiquary has described the grants of new charters to the town by Charles II, and the reform of the corporation in 1835. Of the jubilees celebrated in the town since the days of Garrick to honour the memory of the poet, many records exist, and their barren history has been often told. The purchase by the nation of the birthplace in Henley Street, and of New Place with its gardens, and the erection of the memorial buildings on the river-bank, are fresh in the memory of literary students, and are no unworthy, although in themselves necessarily inadequate, testimonies of a nation's gratitude to Stratford for having nurtured its king of poets.

The origin of the town and its development in the sixteenth and early seventeenth centuries alone afford a profitable study to the lover of Shakespeare. But even while studying them, it is useless to estimate exactly how much the dramatist owed to Stratford. We could point out in the various lists of the town's inhabitants the immortal names of Fluellen and Bardolf, of John Page and Thomas Ford, of Perkes and of Peto, and many more confirmations than appear in the foregoing pages of Aubrey's statement

THE CHANCEL OF STRATFORD CHURCH.

that "he did gather the humours of men daily wherever he came." We might depict Shakespeare seeking inspiration for the sylvan scenes of *As You Like It* beneath the trees of the Warwickshire Forest of Arden. We might

press the theory that makes Lord Carew the lord of *Taming of the Shrew* and Clopton House the scene of Kit Sly's illusion. But it is wiser to take a larger view, and to be content to marvel how, in the aspect of the town and country, fair as the latter was and is, or how in the petty details of Stratford daily life, his mighty genius found adequate nourishment. It is vain to endeavour to solve this mystery, or to strive to indicate either in "the world of living men," or in "wood, and stream, and field, and hill, and ocean,"

All he had loved and moulded into thought.

THE END

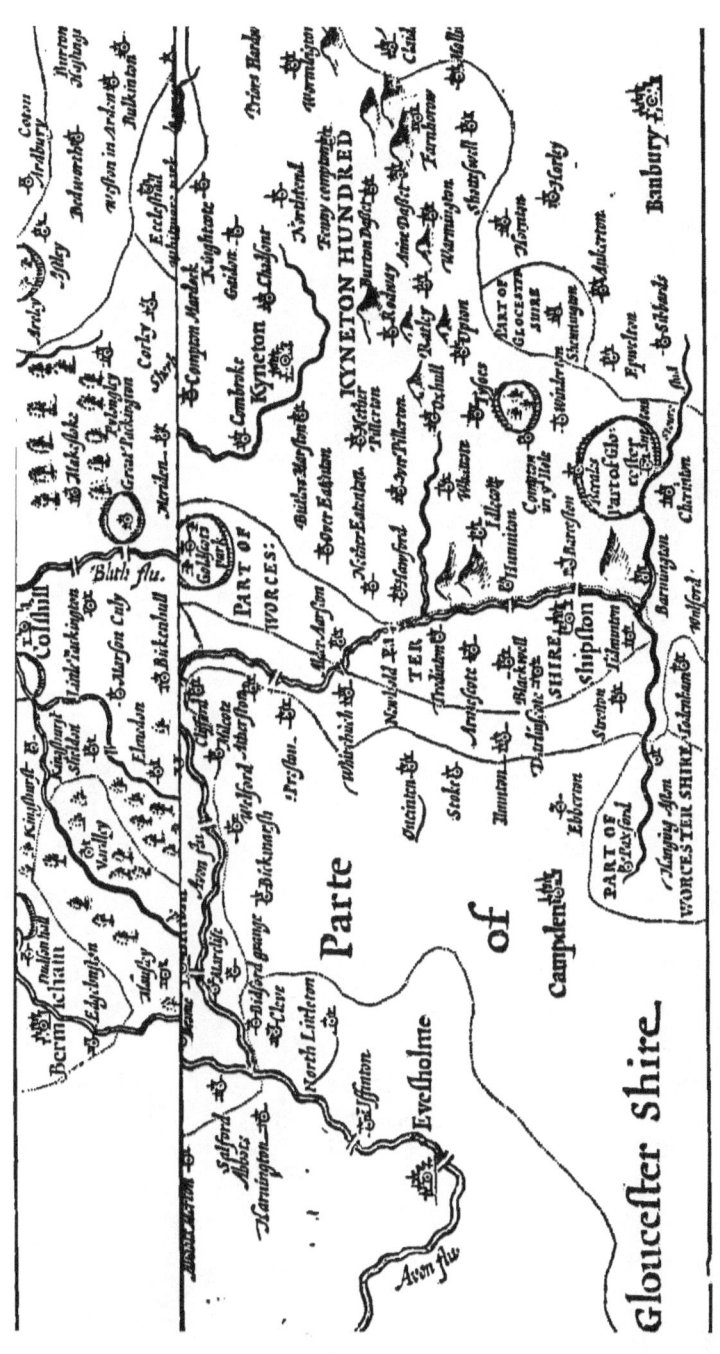

The Neighbourhood of Stratford, from Speed's 'Map of Warwickshire,' 1610.

www.ingramcontent.com/pod-product-compliance
Lightning Source LLC
Chambersburg PA
CBHW030746250426
43672CB00028B/1066